UNTIDY

THE BLOGS ON RUMSFELD

SELECTED AND
INTRODUCED BY

Tom Sumner

William, James & Co.

For B.J.J. Everything for B.J.J.

—T.M.S.

Publisher   Jim Leisy (james_leisy@wmjasco.com)
Cover Photo   Department of Defense photo by R.D. Ward
Proofreader   Brenda Jones

Printed in the U.S.A.

William, James & Co. is an imprint of Franklin, Beedle & Associates, Inc.

Library of Congress Cataloging-in-Publication
data available from the publisher.

ISBN 1-59028-047-4

CONTENTS

Preface

x

Part One
The Stuff of Rumsfeld
1

Part Two
The Bloggers' Rumsfeld
25

CONTENTS

CONTENTS

PREFACE

About This Series

When I was a writing teacher, I struggled to get more writing from my students. More writing, I figured, was more thinking, and then more learning. But most of my students claimed to dislike writing, so I tried to think of ways to make writing fun so I'd see more of it. Turn on the spigot—more, I told myself, was better.

I can't be the only one awed by the blogging phenomenon, since most blogging is writing, that thing I always thought everyone tried to avoid. Yet I watch the number of weblogs rise (a year ago, Technorati, the weblog tracking site, tracked 2.5 million blogs; as I write this it is tracking 8.7 million) and just think back to the days of trying to coerce students to write more.

And now—amazingly—there seems to be no end to how popular writing will become.

I'm not a writing teacher anymore; my career switch has turned me into an editor, and though I still love to see that spigot as it gets turned on higher and higher, I also have an urge to give it direction. Good blogs are updated frequently, and older posts slip off into the archives, out of sight for visitors, unless they are overcome by an urge to click around on old dates. No one will ever have time to read all this output, but the Informed Citizen Series will try to get some of the good writing done on the blogs to stick around.

Writing and Democracy: Political Blogs

Adam Gopnik, staff writer for the *New Yorker* magazine, has also been thinking about writing, the Internet, and democracy. According to the web site for the College Board's Forum 2004 in Chicago, Gopnik participated in a panel discussion and "described how the bloggers and the massive quantity of political discussion that took place on the Internet also gave him a renewed faith in the power of writing. 'I remember 10 or 15 years ago, there was this notion that language itself, written language, was just vanishing from the world and we were going into a world of sound bites and visuals,' said Gopnik. 'But if you think about it, the Internet has proven to be above all a medium of writing.'"

Blogs can be about anything, but reading political blogs—whether they're highlighting stories major media put at the back of the newspaper or relegated to 10 seconds on the newscast, or breaking into rants and heavily opinionated commentary that would never be found in major news outlets, or sticking with a story that has fallen off the radar of other media, or just offering a clipped sentence that directs you to a news item that just might need your attention— does have a way of making you feel like more of a citizen. In an interview with Amy Goodman in March 2005, Juan Cole, former journalist and professor of Middle Eastern Studies at the University of Michigan, said this about the importance of his blog, *Informed Comment*:

After September 11 . . . I felt a great many ignorant opinions were being expressed in our mass media by people who really couldn't even pronounce the names correctly and had no idea what they were talking about. And it annoyed me, having spent a long time in the region and having studied it professionally. And in the old days before the rise of the Internet, it was hard to get one's voice out. People think, well, an academic has some sort of special access, but no. I think a lot of journalists were convinced that academics can't write straight, and you should keep them away from the public if at all possible. So, I couldn't get my op-eds published. And my credentials really meant nothing in the journalistic world. It was only once I started keeping the weblog and commenting on al Qaeda and the development of the war on terror and then especially the Iraq war that the journalists started reading me for information, and I often could get access through Arabic sources on the Internet or in the media to a texture and detail of information that wasn't available in the west.

Of course, not all bloggers come to blogging with the extensive background of Professor Cole, but they do come with something to say and a desire to put it in writing, and with that a desire to spread information and hold an audience. And holding the audience is the whole game; blogs that are not engaging and accurate tend to disappear.

About This Book

I created this book to tell the story of Secretary of Defense Donald Rumsfeld through the eyes of his blogging critics. I intend the blog posts here to present a collage of critical commentary, some of it lengthy and thoughtful, some of it quick and to the point, and some of it whimsical. I wanted two readers to come to this book: the one who already reads blogs but wants to go back and see what was missed while reading all the other good blogs (most of these posts I hadn't noticed the first time around, by the way; only by researching did I come across much of this material for the first time), and the reader who does not already read blogs but wants to take a look at what the Internet has been up to. OK, there is a third reader: the one predisposed to disliking Rumsfeld, and who wants to cover more ground in that regard.

My Ax

I do have an ax to grind. Please note the word *critics* in the previous section. There are many biographies and favorable stories told of our Secretary of Defense. Midge Decter's *Rumsfeld: A Personal Portrait* and Jeffrey A. Krames' *The Rumsfeld Way: The Leadership Wisdom of a Battle-Hardened Maverick* are two examples of biographies that give official portraits of Rumsfeld as a True American Hero. Also, Rumsfeld's views and positions are generally given deference in press conferences and Sunday-morning news shows, not to mention bloggers not represented in this book. Many people—perhaps you or some of your friends, neighbors, or relatives—are partial to Rumsfeld and uninterested in hearing of his perceived failings. I and the other writers featured here, however, take a different position, and if you do not care to read dissent from the official story, and the basis for that dissent, then this book will certainly not be for you.

Acknowledgments

Were it not for all the good bloggers featured here, there would be no book. They posted these great posts, and when I asked them to allow for their reprinting, they graciously agreed. I'd like to list them all by name, but wait—I already have: please take some time to read up on them in the "About the Bloggers" section at the back of this book, and visit their blogs when you have the chance. You will not be sorry you did. While you're at it, be sure to click on the blogrolls, those listings of other recommended blogs that appear on their sites. When you do, you'll find anywhere from dozens to hundreds of other excellent blogs, many of whose posts deserve wider readership.

I'd also like to thank publisher Jim Leisy for letting me proceed with this series and understanding it will be a long, hard slog, but I know in the end we'll have much to show for our hard work. Joel Preston Smith gave "The Stuff of Rumsfeld" the reading it needed. Barbara O'Brien showed me what form a book like this might have, and Jack Miles' and Cynthia Kirk's encouraging words about the effort have been a great contribution. Finally, thank you John Harris for showing me my first blog—and many other good ones since.

—T.M.S., April 2005

PART ONE

THE STUFF OF RUMSFELD

IN APRIL OF 2003, SADDAM was gone. The Iraqi people had gotten what the Bush administration had claimed was their due—freedom from a tyrant, Saddam Hussein. The government of the United States promised the world that the real search for the much-hyped and much feared weapons of mass destruction could begin, now that the United Nations weapons inspectors were gone.[1] And for a period of a few days or weeks, there was tentative hope. Maybe the bombing was over; maybe the loss of life would be minimal. Maybe the people of Iraq would embrace the U.S. as liberators. Maybe history was wrong about occupying forces, and some grand mix of American ingenuity and compassion would annihilate the pervading pessimism felt by those of us who had opposed this invasion.

Something very different was observed. The early signs were that Iraq was in a state of something far beyond what we think of as freedom—there was utter chaos. Looting was rampant. Famously, the National Museum of Iraq was looted, but the raiding of hospitals and even people's homes made the situation intolerable. With no space in the morgue, children who had died in the invasion were buried in the back yard of the Saddam Hospital for Children, and the Red Cross reported that just three hospitals of the thirty-two in Baghdad were open, and those were not fully operational. [2]

Reports of the horror came frequently and brutally. Bodies stacked in piles. Iraqis needing emergency care were left unattended due to lack of electricity and clean water. There were car-jackings, bombings, and kidnappings. For me, though, I was haunted by one BBC interview I heard with a British woman who had lived in Iraq for more than 20 years, and who had spent the days since the fall of the old regime sequestered inside, fearing that if she ventured out she would come back to find her home ransacked. She was asked about life under Saddam and responded that she never had paid attention to politics, but there was one restriction the Iraqi government had tried to impose: it had tried to force her to become an Iraqi citizen as a requirement for continued residency, but the World Court ruled against this overreaching of government authority, and that was the end of that. The reporter then asked her if she was not relieved to have freedom from the oppressive Baathist government of Saddam. With Iraq in anarchy, her response said it all: "What freedom?"

Secretary of Defense Donald Rumsfeld had an answer for her. In the midst of these days, he delivered one of his most memorable quotes: "Freedom's untidy, and free people are free to make mistakes and commit crimes and do bad things," the secretary said. "They're also free to live their lives and do wonderful things. And that's what's going to happen here."[3] It was the first half of the quote that drew attention, the part that forced us to consider freedom and chaos as somehow inextricably bound together.

As an addendum to his statement, Rumsfeld came as close to shrugging his shoulders in language as I believe anyone can. "Stuff happens," he said. Freedom, criminal activity, wonderful things—Stuff Happens.

Many months later, in late October of 2004, with the U.S. military operations mired in Iraq due to a well-organized and well-armed resistance to occupation, the looting story resurfaced. A large stash of explosives—380 tons of RDX, enough, apparently, to bring down more than 700,000 planes in the manner of the Lockerbie, Scotland, terrorist bombing—was looted from a site at Al Qaqaa when Baghdad fell.

Since United Nations weapons inspectors had kept the site secure for more than a decade prior to the invasion, questions about Rumsfeld's plan for post-war occupation were revisited. Before the war, Rumsfeld had severely criticized Army Chief of Staff General Eric Shinseki, who was removed from his position after publicly saying the post-war occupation of Iraq would require several hundred thousand troops, instead of the 100,000 Rumsfeld and Deputy Secretary of Defense Paul Wolfowitz claimed were necessary. Rumsfeld made it very clear: "The idea that it would take several hundred thousand U.S. forces," he said in February of 2003, "I think is far off the mark." Clearly, though, the light force used to take Iraq has been overstretched when it has come to keeping Iraq secure.

Rumsfeld's late-in-life celebrity status—achieved in part by the mystique of becoming U.S. Secretary of Defense for a second time in 2001, after a 24-year hiatus—came after a long period of building connections in Washington, D.C., in the public and private sectors. After graduating from Princeton in 1954, Rumsfeld served as a U.S. Navy pilot and flight instructor from 1954–1957. In fact, his four years of active duty and several years after that in the Reserve—having retired with a rank of Captain in 1989—give him almost unrivaled military experience in the high levels of the George W. Bush administration, an administration that has orchestrated two major military invasions and occupations in the area of the Middle East.

While in the Reserves, first in the Ready Reserve (until 1975), then in the Standby Reserve (until 1989), Rumsfeld pursued a career that mixed politics and executive experience in private corporations. He was elected to the U.S. House of Representatives in 1962 and served until 1969, when he left Congress to join the Nixon administration as Director of the Office of Economic Opportunity and Assistant to the President until 1971, when he became Counselor to the President and Director of the Economic Stabilization Program. In 1973, as Watergate began to materialize as a bona fide scandal, he departed Washington to serve as U.S. ambassador to NATO in Brussels. Rumsfeld has been part of every Republican administration since. Some of the highlights include serving as the youngest Secretary of Defense for Gerald Ford from 1975–1977 and acting as Special Presidential Envoy to the Middle East for President Reagan from 1983–1984. It was in that capacity that he visited Iraq in 1983 to let Saddam Hussein know that the U.S. was ready for friendly relations with Iraq, even though Saddam had been accused of using chemical weapons in the Iran-Iraq war raging at the time. A photo of Rumsfeld shaking hands with Saddam Hussein during that visit is ubiquitous; nearly every political web site has featured it at some time.

Since 1977, Rumsfeld has moved fairly freely between private industry and the White House. In that year he became Chief Executive Officer of G.D. Searle & Co., a pharmaceutical giant. He was credited with turning around the fortunes of that company, and he stayed with Searle until 1985, when he went into private business. In 1990 he became C.E.O. of General Instrument Corporation, and from 1993–2001, he was C.E.O. of Gilead Sciences, Inc., another pharmaceutical giant.

There are plenty of details that could be pored over here—but I have to confess that my first reaction, when I read such a biography, is to wonder how one man can accumulate so many important-sounding titles. 1983, for example, seems to have been an especially busy one for Rumsfeld. That was the year he served simultaneously as a Member of the President's General Advisory Committee on Arms Control, Special Presidential Envoy on the Law of the Sea Treaty, Senior Advisor to the President's Panel on Strategic Systems, Member of the U.S. Joint Advisory Commission on U.S.-Japan Relations, and Special Presidential Envoy to the Middle East, according to his official biography.[4]

One of the more curious aspects of Rumsfeld's biography is his extensive experience in the pharmaceutical industry. Why, you have to wonder, does the Secretary of Defense have so much background in pharmaceuticals? It's a question worth trying to answer (indeed, the Rumsfeld-pharmaceuticals-chemical weapons connection has been investigated[5]), but the other logical question is, since he operated as C.E.O., how did he run those companies, and what is his executive style?

At Searle, Rumsfeld was credited with saving the company by decentralizing its headquarters and selling off poorly performing divisions. It is also interesting that Searle, before hiring Rumsfeld, was having difficulty getting federal approval to market aspartame, a sweetener the Food and Drug Administration would not approve because of its link to brain tumors in laboratory rats. Rumsfeld, according to Patty Wood-Allott, a former Searle sales representative, promised to "call in his markers" to get FDA approval for aspartame. Presumably, Rumsfeld would call upon his connections in Washington to help Searle land FDA approval. In 1981—with Rumsfeld in the middle of his tenure as head of Searle and the newly-elected President Reagan— aspartame was approved by FDA Commissioner Arthur Hill Hayes.[6] To this day, allegations of the dangers of aspartame swirl (specifically, it is thought that aspartame might be toxic because the body converts one of its ingredients, methanol, into formaldehyde), though the majority of scientists regard it as safe. Certainly, there has been no aspartame-related public health crisis in the 24 years since its approval, but the circumstances of its approval—and Rumsfeld's apparent influence—give a glimpse into the intermingling of scientific research, government bureaucracy, and corporate influence that we have come to associate with Donald Rumsfeld and the George W. Bush administration in general. Aspartame languishes for years after its discovery in 1955, Searle seeks FDA approval for it, Rumsfeld is hired as C.E.O., aspartame gets approved by the FDA. Stuff Happens.

In fact, blurring the line between what was once considered the public domain (Social Security, health, defense, etc.) and private venture (selling and buying of everything else) is a defining feature of the Bush administration. In the case of Rumsfeld, this is praised by Americans for Tax Reform, headed by Grover Norquist, a prominent and influential member of the Republican Party:

> . . . an internal memorandum by Secretary of the Army Thomas E. White on October 4th said, "The Army must focus its energies and talents on our core competencies—functions we perform better than anybody else…and obtain other needed products or services from the private sector where it makes sense."
>
> "Rumsfeld and White should be praised for their hard work to reduce the size of the bureaucracy and reduce squandering valuable resources where they are not needed. If approved, this will furthermore serve to save taxpayers from wasteful spending on projects that the Pentagon does not require for its mission," Grover Norquist, president of Americans for Tax Reform, stated.
>
> Privatization would save millions of taxpayer dollars without affecting the Army or Defense Department's mission. The Department of the Army currently employs 1.3 million, of which around 220,000 are civilians. The privatization would affect almost 155,000 civilian and 59,000 military personnel.
>
> The Army's reorganization is only a portion [of] what the Bush administration is seeking. In total, the administration would like to see up to 425,000 government jobs up for competition in the private

sector. These moves will allow the military to focus towards the war on terrorism and emerging threats.

"Hopefully these changes will be implemented without delay, as to not further impede upon the Defense Department's current missions," Norquist added.[7]

In other words, private corporations will provide services previously thought of as the responsibility of the government. Norquist is confident of the tax savings this plan will provide, but nowhere does he bring up any of the obvious holes in the theory of shrinking government by privatizing the military. It almost seems too obvious to point out that contracts awarded to private companies are paid for by—who else?—taxpayers. So instead of turning tax money over to the Pentagon to administer and fund the military, the Pentagon takes that tax money and finds private corporations who provide the same services and who operate at a profit. It is not what we otherwise know as free enterprise, where a consumer selects and buys a pair of shoes, for example. In the case of the military, the consumer (the taxpayer) hands over money to the Pentagon, which then goes shopping with it. There's always been this component—factories have been wisely retooled to produce for the military—but currently there are corporations that would not exist were it not for the contracts they receive from the U. S. military, which raises the question of what privatization of the military even means.

In present-day military operations, latrines are cleaned and food is served by private contractors. It sounds reasonable on the surface—let the soldiers do what they're supposed to do in frontline fighting and peacekeeping duties, and leave the other hassles of conducting a war to private companies who can provide those services. In reality, the frugality of privatizing is not so simple, as Nicholas von Hoffman wrote in *Harper's Magazine*:

> The rationale for privatizing American war making is that corporate warriors can do the job for less. But no proof exists that hiring private firms is cheaper. In theory, private contracting creates competitive pressure to reduce costs, but in practice the bidding process can be so opaque and distorted by favoritism that it becomes an empty formality. Many of the large rebuilding contracts in Iraq were made under no-bid or "emergency" conditions. The starkest example of this crony competition is Kellogg Brown & Root's $7 billion contract to restore the Iraqi oil industry. The Army told the *New York Times* last June that KBR was awarded the contract without competition because it was the only company that fulfilled the criteria set out by the Army's "contingency plan." The contingency plan, of course, was written by KBR itself. In the grand tradition pioneered by Boss Tweed, contractor waste abounds. Last year, Halliburton alone was found to have overcharged the military roughly $1 per gallon for tens of millions of gallons of gasoline and $16 million for feeding soldiers at a base in Kuwait.[8]

Von Hoffman further points out that private corporations, unlike the Pentagon, are not subject to the Freedom of Information Act, so they may evade that form of oversight—oversight that very likely would cut down on wasteful spending. Still, information does occasionally leak, as in the CNN report that private security contractors can be paid up to $1,500 per day.[9]

It's quite likely that contracting out this work saves nothing in taxpayer money. Even though privatizing effectively drives down labor costs in some areas (in food service, for example), corporations have their own problems with waste, corruption, and bloated C.E.O. salaries. Privatization actually involves more government oversight of the process— or at least it should, as in the case of the unaccounted-for $8.8 billion that has disappeared, somewhere, into private companies doing contract work in Iraq, according to an August 2004 audit.[10]

Privatization, though a key component of Rumsfeld's vision of a stripped-down, cost-effective military, is not mentioned in his 2002 article, "Transforming the Military," in *Foreign Affairs*. In that piece, Rumsfeld contrasts the modern military with the military of the Cold War era, which was so focused on a threat coming from the Soviet Union. These days, Rumsfeld says, the U.S. faces new threats:

> First, wars in the twenty-first century will increasingly require all elements of national power: economic, diplomatic, financial, law enforcement, intelligence, and both overt and covert military operations. Clausewitz said, "War is the continuation of politics by other means." In this century, more of those means may not be military.
>
> Second, the ability of forces to communicate and operate seamlessly on the battlefield will be critical to success. In Afghanistan, we saw composite teams of U.S. special forces on the ground, working with Navy, Air Force, and Marine Corps pilots in the sky to identify targets and coordinate the timing of air strikes—with devastating consequences for the enemy. The lesson of this war is

that effectiveness in combat will depend heavily on "jointness"—that is, the ability of the different branches of our military to communicate and coordinate their efforts on the battlefield. But achieving jointness in wartime requires building it in peacetime. We must train like we fight and fight like we train.

Third, our policy in this war of accepting help from any country, on a basis comfortable for its government, and allowing that country to characterize how it is helping (instead of our creating that characterization for it), is enabling us to maximize both other countries' cooperation and our effectiveness against the enemy.

Fourth, wars can benefit from coalitions of the willing, to be sure, but they should not be fought by committee. The mission must determine the coalition, the coalition must not determine the mission, or else the mission will be dumbed down to the lowest common denominator.

Fifth, defending the United States requires prevention and sometimes preemption. It is not possible to defend against every threat, in every place, at every conceivable time. Defending against terrorism and other emerging threats requires that we take the war to the enemy. The best—and, in some cases, the only—defense is a good offense.

Sixth, rule nothing out—including ground forces. The enemy must understand that we will use every means at our disposal to defeat them, and that we are prepared to make whatever sacrifices are necessary to achieve victory.

Seventh, getting U.S. special forces on the ground early dramatically increases the effectiveness of an air campaign. Afghanistan showed that

> precision-guided bombs from the sky are much
> more effective if we get boots and eyes on the
> ground to tell the bombers exactly where to aim.[11]

Reading this Rumsfeld document can leave a feeling of great dread for the future, one that seemingly will have nothing to offer but threats, pre-emption, and retaliation from and against a world populated with enemies of the United States. But given his topic, he puts forth a lofty design for the military that includes all of the above, plus a call for the military to "place greater emphasis on deterrence in four critical theaters, backed by the ability to swiftly defeat two aggressors at the same time, while preserving the option for one massive counteroffensive to occupy an aggressor's capital and replace its regime." He also calls for "increase[d] funding for defense of the U.S. homeland and overseas bases by 47 percent; for programs to deny enemies sanctuary by 157 percent; for programs to ensure long-distance power projection in hostile areas by 21 percent; for programs to harness information technology by 125 percent; for programs to attack enemy information networks and defend our own by 28 percent; and for programs to strengthen U.S. space capabilities by 145 percent." Far from the rhetoric of Norquist, this is a flight away from reduced spending. The closest Rumsfeld comes here to mentioning privatization at all is his echo of the rant that wasteful government can never compete with the thrift of the private sector: "We must promote a more entrepreneurial approach: one that encourages people to be proactive, not reactive, and to behave less like bureaucrats and more like venture capitalists."

So which is the real Rumsfeld military? The one that wants to increase spending on all fronts, or the one that wants to be a lean machine, operating with great thrift and looking to the private sector for inspiration? In fact, since the beginning of Rumsfeld's current tenure as Secretary of Defense, the budget for the Pentagon has increased every year, with the September 11 attacks commonly used to justify the need for pouring more money into defense. According to Ron Suskind's book, *The Price of Loyalty*, however, in early 2001 Rumsfeld requested a defense-spending increase of between $255 billion and $842 billion over the course of five years, based not on a stateless terrorist threat, but on the threat of rogue states acquiring weapons of mass destruction.

The Pentagon budget now is at a 50-year high, though in the face of enormous deficits and growing U.S. debt, defense spending—previously slated to be curtailed—continues to rise. The $419 billion defense budget President Bush has proposed for 2006 does not include funding for the wars in Afghanistan and Iraq, and costs in Iraq alone are expected to be $100 billion.[12] The expense of wars in Afghanistan and Iraq is currently at about $300 billion, a figure that naturally continues to rise. Apparently, talking honestly about these numbers is not always in your best interest. In 2002, White House economic adviser Larry Lindsey estimated the Iraq war would cost between $100 and $200 billion. Depending on what account you read, Lindsey was either forced to resign or fired outright for publicly making that estimate, considered far too high at the time.

Where does all this money, overseen by Rumsfeld, go? Again, according to Nicholas von Hoffman, the latrine cleaners and oil industry workers are real, but in fact, about 20,000 of the soldiers fighting in Iraq have been working for private contractors. The Abu Ghraib prison interrogation/abuse/torture—all of this vocabulary has been applied to it—

was carried out partly by employees of CACI (California Analysis Center Incorporated) and Titan, two private contractors. Privatizing interrogation has been falsely justified, once again, as a cost-cutting scheme, but the one real "benefit" to this plan is that private corporations do not sign international treaties (and neither are they subject to the laws of the Geneva Conventions), and private interrogators are not part of the military chain of command. That is, they cannot be court-martialed. This all serves to complicate the prosecution of these cases.[13]

The war in Iraq has come to define Rumsfeld's career. As a signer of The Project for a New American Century (PNAC)[14], the think tank that in the 1990s encouraged an aggressive new direction for U.S. foreign policy, he was a leader in calling for regime change in Iraq long before the September 11 attacks. This group—counting Vice President Dick Cheney, Deputy Secretary of Defense Paul Wolfowitz, Florida Governor Jeb Bush, brother of the President, and Deputy National Security Adviser Elliott Abrams among its members—advocates for the U.S. to assert itself as a kind of benevolent dictator of the world, using military might when necessary, but by all means destabilizing and overthrowing governments perceived to be obstructing U.S. interests. Their documents make it clear that China is potentially the greatest threat for becoming a world superpower to rival the strength of the U.S., but the Middle East is perceived as pivotal because maintaining a reliable supply of oil is key for the U.S. to continue as the dominant superpower.

Many catchphrases have sprung up to rebut such thinking. One, the "no blood/war for oil" cant, focuses on the issue of resources. Another, "American Empire," focuses on PNAC's perceived intent to take over the world. Yet another, "neo-cons" or "neo-conservatism" (or, historically, "neo-liberalism") focuses on the philosophy of the organization, and in fact, this is the wording the group's members use to describe themselves. All of these phrases, while pointing out essential truths, somehow fall flat in the face of the power the PNAC members represent. Their documents, a quite radical collection of writings, could never be taken seriously were it not for that power. Dick Cheney's paper, "Defense Strategy for the 1990s," which called for the United States to "maintain its overwhelming military superiority and prevent new rivals from rising up to challenge it on the world stage," and also stated that the United States must be not "more powerful, or most powerful, but that it must be absolutely powerful," as David Armstrong put it,[15] was not embraced when first submitted in 1993. But since Cheney became Vice President, and especially since the September 11 attacks, the plan has become policy. Its themes are echoed in many PNAC documents, including "Rebuilding America's Defenses," dated September 2000. This document contains an oft-cited passage—a favorite among September 11 conspiracy-theorists—claiming that "the process of transformation, even if it brings revolutionary change, is likely to be a long one, absent some catastrophic and catalyzing event—like a new Pearl Harbor."[16]

The PNAC group has proved to be nothing if not resilient. One notable example was an egg-on-your-face story printed in *The Guardian*, the left-leaning London newspaper, from June of 2003, quoting Paul Wolfowitz in a speech in Asia. He was asked why the U.S. invaded Iraq, while North Korea was also pursuing weapons programs, and may even be a nuclear state. Iraq was chosen, the paper reported Wolfowitz as saying, because "the country swims on a sea of oil." It turned out later that the reporter was quoting Wolfowitz wildly out of context. The point he was making in that speech was not that the U.S. wanted Iraq's oil, you see, but rather that oil put the Iraq regime in a position of wealth (to build weapons rapidly, presumably, or something) while North Korea was resource-poor and therefore economically unviable, so the U.S. could better afford to allow North Korea to just self-destruct, while it was clear that the Iraqi regime, if left alone, could flourish. The story was an example of what seems to be a recurring theme for neoconservatives of the Bush administration: a prominent neocon seems to be trapped in some damning situation, outed once and for all as a ruthless, unscrupulous lout, then some new information comes out or the story just goes away, and the next thing you know, the person in the story comes back unscathed.

If the Wolfowitz example gives a small taste of this, Rumsfeld's career since invading Iraq has been a feast. We saw it very early on, during the initial military invasion, when there were one or two difficult days for the U.S. military. The war plan was being questioned, and Rumsfeld looked uneasy as his strategy of using light force on the ground hit some snags. When it became merely easy for the U.S. military instead of a cakewalk, Rumsfeld was on the ropes. After it became clear that "easy" was as difficult as it was going to get, Rumsfeld was back in stride.

Since that time, Rumsfeld has appeared to be on the mat several times, most particularly over the direction he's given on handling prisoners. In spring of 2004, photos emerged of Iraqi prisoners held at Abu Ghraib, the most notorious prison of the Saddam regime, now in control of the U.S. military. Seymour Hersh reported in the *New Yorker* that round-ups of Iraqi citizens had been ordered to try to collect information on a growing Iraqi insurgency. The prisoners had never been charged with anything, but they were being held, abused, and tortured in attempts to get information from them. According to Hersh, the direction for this program, and other programs at Guantanamo Bay in Cuba and in Afghanistan, came from all the way up the chain of command to Rumsfeld. Other stories about suspects being taken to other countries to be tortured have emerged since then, including the story of *Time*'s Canadian newsmaker of the year for 2004, Maher Arar. According to *Time*, Arar, Syrian-born and a naturalized Canadian citizen since 1991, was traveling through JFK airport in New York on September 26, 2002, on his way back from a vacation to visit his wife's family in Tunisia when he was picked up, detained, and interrogated for 10 days in a Brooklyn detention center. *Time* picks up the story:

> Then, in the middle of the night, he was put into shackles and spirited away via Jordan to Syria, a country he hadn't been to in 16 years, despite the fact that he was a naturalized Canadian citizen traveling on a Canadian passport en route to Canada.
>
> Arar ended up in a dark, 1-m[eter] by 2-m[eter] cell he calls the "grave" in the Syrian military intelligence agency's Palestine branch in Damascus. He was held there without charge for 10 months and

10 days. During his first two weeks, he claims, he was interrogated about people he had known in Canada, sometimes for 18 hours at a time, and tortured. One punishment, he says, was repeated lashings with a 5-cm black metal cable on his palms, wrists, lower back and hips. The mental ordeal was also brutal, he said in November 2003 at one of the most dramatic press conferences ever televised in Canada. "The second and third days were the worst," he told the world that day. "I could hear other prisoners being tortured, and screaming." During his first week in prison, he says, he falsely confessed that he had received military training in Afghanistan.[17]

All of this has put Rumsfeld very much on the hotseat. A lawsuit dismissed in Germany in February 2005 had been pursuing him for war crimes, but as quickly as that lawsuit was dropped, eight men who said they had been tortured filed a suit in federal court against Rumsfeld. Still, there does not seem to be any chance President Bush will ever relieve him of his duties, though several prominent conservatives and neo-conservatives (including William Kristol, chairman of PNAC), have publicly announced they have no confidence in Rumsfeld.

It's likely that dismissing Rumsfeld would not have much effect on U.S. foreign policy. Any replacement for Rumsfeld would need to be in step with the PNAC cabal that holds so much sway in the Bush administration.[18] Criticism from conservatives focuses on Rumsfeld's inability to carry out the plan—as damaged goods, someone associated with torture and a quagmire in Iraq—not on his ideological bent. The plan, as envisioned by PNAC, calls for regime change in Iraq, but also Iran and Syria. In January

2005, Seymour Hersh wrote in the *New Yorker* about the current state of Pentagon operations in Iran, including secretly sending in forces to identify possible future military targets. "In my interviews," Hersh wrote, "I was repeatedly told [by intelligence and military officials] that the next strategic target was Iran."[19]

In December 2004, when in Kuwait to speak to and meet members of the National Guard serving in Iraq, Rumsfeld fielded an unscripted question from Specialist Thomas Wilson, who asked why the armor on military vehicles was inadequate to withstand many of the attacks of Iraqi insurgent fighters. Rumsfeld answered, "You go to war with the Army you have, not the Army you might want or wish to have," and later said that the production of armored vehicles was the result of manufacturers' running behind schedule (a statement refuted by the manufacturers in question). That exchange put a spotlight on many of the frustrations Americans have felt about the war in Iraq: an invasion that was unnecessary for national security, a failure to secure sites containing explosives that might be used against our military, a failure to win over the hearts and minds of the Iraqi people (as may have been accomplished by properly securing the country, firmly taking a stance against torture, and putting an end to all looting in the direct aftermath of the invasion), the inability of the private sector to fill the needs of the military as designed by Rumsfeld, and the sense that the soldiers on the ground pay a much higher price for these failures than anyone issuing orders.

We don't know if Rumsfeld feels that mistakes have been made. Certainly, if he does feel that way, he has never let it be known. The pattern has been one of revelation of damning information, followed by pronouncements that it's the fault of the media for revealing information that would be better kept out of public earshot. In February 2005 the *Washington Post* reported that the Pentagon created the Strategic Support Branch, a secret spy unit. Its job is to provide intelligence to military Special Operations units. We don't know too much about it just now because Rumsfeld had to reinterpret U.S. law in order to form this unit without telling anyone about it, including Congress. According to the *Post*, this unit would recruit outside agents, including notorious figures whose "links to the U.S. government would be embarrassing if disclosed."

It's such a classic Rumsfeld story, one that could bring down his whole career, but won't. Reinterpreting law, operating undercover, employing outside agents—really, it's just another telling of the same tale that's been told about the handling of prisoners and enemies in the "war on terror" Rumsfeld has been put in charge of.

So even if he could, I don't think Rumsfeld would roll back time and unmake his decision to create the Strategic Support Branch, and neither would he take back any of his decisions on handling prisoners of this war. Wouldn't change Abu Ghraib or Guantanamo, or those operations that lift suspects from one country and deport them to other countries that practice torture. Iraq, in this rollback of time, would be again invaded and taken over, then allowed to be looted by its own people. Rumsfeld's military would be equipped just as it is because "you go to war with the Army you have." Afghanistan would be left as a stepchild project to

Iraq, never fully secured outside of Kabul, its capital. Following September 11, when Afghanistan was the logical country for retaliation, he would still respond that Iraq would be better because "there are no good targets in Afghanistan."[20] PNAC, with its aggressive obsession to militarily take over Iraq, would still count Rumsfeld among its members, and the cozy relations between wealth and the military—so reminiscent of the Soviet Union at its peak—would still flourish. And, to artificially sweeten it all—or perhaps to preserve these events in formaldehyde—aspartame would again be pushed into the marketplace. None of it would be undone; Rumsfeld has every appearance of a man with no regrets, and to undo any of this would betray his resolve, would betray his strong sense of blamelessness. And anyway, you can't just turn back time and pretend that none of this stuff ever happened.

Notes for "The Stuff of Rumsfeld"

1. In hindsight, given that their findings were ignored by the intelligence reports used to justify the U.S. invasion of Iraq—and the subsequent multiple admissions that no weapons of mass destruction were in the hands of the Iraq military, or even in development—the work of the U.N. weapons inspectors may be illuminated somewhat by Scott Ritter, weapons inspector from 1991–1998. He has said the weapons-inspection process was used "as a Trojan horse to insert intelligence capabilities into Iraq, which were not approved by the United Nations and which did not facilitate the disarmament process, [but] were instead focused on the security of Saddam Hussein and military targets." (Fox News interview with David Asman, 12 September 2002, available online at http://www.foxnews.com/story/0,2933,62916,00.html).

2. Smucker, Philip and Michael Smith, "Hospital looters stealing incubators and drugs." *Telegraph | News | Hospital looters stealing incubators and drugs*. 12 April 2003. http://www.telegraph.co.uk/news/main.jhtml? xml=/news/2003/04/12/whosp12.xml. 3 February 2005.

3. Loughlin, Sean. "Rumsfeld on looting in Iraq: 'Stuff happens'" *CNN.com - Rumsfeld on looting in Iraq: 'Stuff happens' - April 12, 2003*. 12 April 2003. http://www.cnn.com/2003/US/ 04/11/sprj.irq.pentagon/. 5 April 2005.

4. *Biography - Donald Rumsfeld*. 30 March 2005. http://www.defenselink. mil/bios/rumsfeld.html. 30 March 2005.

5. See, for example, the news release from The Sunshine Project: "And on February 5th [2003], US Secretary of Defense Donald Rumsfeld went a big step further. Rumsfeld, himself a former pharmaceutical industry CEO . . . announced that the US is making plans for the use of such incapacitating biochemical weapons in an invasion of Iraq." 11 February 2003. http://www.sunshine-project.org/publications/pr/pr110203.html. 28 December 2004.

The Sunshine Project report, which has all the earmarks of easily-dismissed conspiracy mongering, actually meshes with Arab press reports that the Iraq Ministry of Health found mustard gas and nerve gas had been usee by the U.S. military during the November 2004 Fallujah offensive (see, for example, "US Troops Reportedly Gassing Fallujah."10 November 2004. *Islam Online - News Section*. http:// islamonline.net/English/News/2004-11/10/article05.shtml).

The U.S. military has officially denied using any banned weapons in Iraq: "The United States categorically denies the use of chemical weapons at anytime in Iraq, which includes the ongoing [November 2004] Fallujah operation," although in April 2003, "Mark-77 fire-bombs, which have a similar effect to napalm, were used against enemy positions in 2003." ("Did the U.S. Use 'Illegal' Weapons in Fallujah?" *Illegal Weapons in Fallujah - US Department of State*. 27 January 2005. http://usinfo.state.gov/media/Archive_Index/Illegal_Weapons_in _Fallujah.html. 30 March 2005.)

6. Evangelista, Arthur M., Alex Constantine, and Gregory Gordon. "History of Aspartame." *History of Aspartame*. 12 March 2004. http:// www.wnho.net/history_of_aspartame.htm. 30 March 2005.

7. Press Release from Americans for Tax Reform. "Rumsfeld, Army Move to Privatize Over 210,000 Employees." *ATR: Press Releases: Rumsfeld, Army Move to Privatize Over 210,000 Employees*. 6 November 2002. http://www.atr.org/pressreleases/2002/110602pr-4.html. 30 March 2005.

8. Von Hoffman, Nicholas. "Contract killers: how privatizing the U.S. military subverts public oversight." *Harper's Magazine: Contract killers:*

how privatizing the U.S. military subverts public oversight. June 2004.
http://www.findarticles.com/p/articles/mi_m1111/is_1849_308/
ai_n6134251. 30 March 2005.

9. CNN.com. "High pay — and high risks — for contractors in Iraq."
*CNN.com - High pay -- and high risks -- for contractors in Iraq - April 2,
2004.* 2 April 2004. http://www.cnn.com/2004/WORLD/meast/04/01/
iraq.contractor/. 5 April 2005.

10. Reuters. "Audit shows $8.8 billion in Iraq funds missing: Coalition
official cites body for lax 'stewardship.'" *Audit shows $8.8 billion in Iraq
funds missing.* 19 August 2004. http://msnbc.msn.com/id/5763483/.
30 March 2005.

11. Rumsfeld, Donald H. "Transforming the Military."*Forein Affairs -
Transforming the Military - Donald Rumsfeld.* May/June 2002. http://
www.foreignaffairs.org/20020501faessay8140/donald-h-rumsfeld/
transforming-the-military.html. 30 March 2005. Reprinted in its
entirety: http://www.pbs.org/wgbh/pages/frontline/shows/missile/etc/
rumsfeld.html.

12. Hess, Pamela. "Pentagon's $419 billion is partial request."*Pentagon's
$419 billion is partial request - (United Press International).* 7 February
2005. http://www.washtimes.com/upi-breaking/20050207-101009-
5328r.htm. 30 March 2005.

13. As reprinted from the *San Franciso Chronicle,* CorpWatch.org posts
this: "We need to face reality," said Peter Singer, an analyst at the
Brookings Institution in Washington and author of the recently released
book, *Corporate Warriors: The Rise of the Privatized Military Industry.*

"While most people have not heard of this industry, it's a $100
billion-per-year business whose largest client is the U.S. government.
But it has virtually no laws, oversight or any public understanding of
how to deal with it," he said.

Singer noted that because of loopholes in international law, employees of private security companies are usually able to escape prosecution
for crimes they commit overseas. Most common crimes occurring
outside the United States are beyond the jurisdiction of American
courts, and many U.S. and U.N. contracts abroad obligate local
governments to give legal immunity to such contractors. (Collier,
Robert. "Iraq: Global Security Firms Fill in as Private Armies."
CorpWatch: Iraq: Global Security Firms Fill in as Private Armies.
28 March 2004. http://www.corpwatch.org/article.php?id=11263.
30 March 2005.)

14. The Project for a New American Century keeps its web site up to date: http://www.newamericancentury.org/.

15. Armstrong, David. "Dick Cheney's song of America: drafting a plan for global dominance." *Harper's Magazine: Dick Cheney's song of America: drafting a plan for global dominance - Criticism.* October 2002. http://www.findarticles.com/p/articles/mi_m1111/is_1829_305/ai_92589441. 30 March 2005.

16. Donnely, Thomas, Donald Kagan, and Gary Schmitt. "Rebuilding America's Defenses," September 2000, p. 51. Available online at http://www.newamericancentury.org/RebuildingAmericasDefenses.pdf.

17. Bryden, Joan and Chris Daniels, "Canadian Newsmakers of the Year." *TIME canada.com.* 2004. http://www.timecanada.com/CNOY/story.adp?year=2004. 30 March 2005.

18. In February 2005, Karen Kwiatkowski, retired US Air Force Lt. Colonel who worked in the office of the Under Secretary of Defense for Policy, Near East South Asia and Special Plans in the Pentagon, stated that the imminent departure of neo-conservative Douglas Feith from the Office of Special Plans was a sign that PNAC influence in the White House was fading. Greg Palast in March 2005 stated that Paul Wolfowitz's and John Bolton's departures from the Pentagon to the World Bank and United Nations, respectively, was also evidence of this phenomenon. With Rumsfeld and Dick Cheney retaining their positions, however, it's difficult to say whether this is an accurate interpretation, and Flynt Leverett, who served as President Bush's senior director for Middle East affairs at the National Security Council from March 2002 to March 2003, stated in a *Democracy Now!* interview in March 2005 that he perceived neo-conservative influence in the White House would continue despite Wolfowitz's and Bolton's departures.

19. Hersh, Seymour M. "The Coming Wars." *New Yorker: Fact.* 17 January 2005. http://newyorker.com/fact/content/?050124fa_fact. 30 March 2005.

20. Reported here and elsewhere: Webb, Justin. "Analysis: Insider's attack rattles Bush." *BBC NEWS | Americas | Analysis: Insider's attack rattles Bush.* 22 March 2004. http://news.bbc.co.uk/2/hi/americas/3559153.stm. 30 March 2005.

P A R T   T W O

THE BLOGGERS' RUMSFELD

A FAVORITE TOPIC AMONG BLOGGERS, RUMSFELD has been written about regularly since the popularity of blogs really began to expand, which conveniently coincided with the beginning of the presidency of George W. Bush.

The following blog entries represent some of the best critical commentary on Rumsfeld that has appeared on the Internet. His professional background, his notable quirks of speech (including his propensity to ask, then answer his own questions), his thinking on the treatment of prisoners, the recurring controversy of his tenure as Secretary of Defense, and his role as architect of the military—it's all here in these bloggers' observations of Rumsfeld.

These entries have been left more or less intact. Note that some typos have been corrected and some sections of text have been cut to keep the focus on the topic at hand. I've included three posts from *Fafblog*, a political/social-satire/parody blog; the other entries are grounded in Rumsfeld's actual words and deeds.

THE ROAD TO SURFDOM

July 12, 2002

www.roadtosurfdom.com

Step aside George Orwell, the master is at work

by Tim Dunlop

George Orwell might have named the practice—doublethink, newspeak—and may have even fictionalized it nicely in *1984*; and Bill Clinton may have asserted some authority in the art when testifying over the Lewinsky affair—especially the bit that went "it depends what your definition of *is* is"; but when it comes to contemptuous political misuse of language and power, Donald Rumsfeld is the real McCoy. This from a press conference given in Brussels:

> The message is that there are no "knowns." There are things we know that we know. There are known unknowns. That is to say there are things that we now know we don't know. But there are also unknown unknowns. There are things we don't know we don't know. So when we do the best we can and we pull all this information together, and we then say well, that's basically what we see as the situation, that is really only the known knowns and the known unknowns. And each year, we discover a few more of those unknown unknowns. . . . There's another way to phrase that and that is that the absence of evidence is not evidence of absence.

LANGUAGE LOG
December 2, 2003
http://itre.cis.upenn.edu/~myl/languagelog

No foot in mouth

by Geoffrey K. Pullum

I'm as much in favor of good plain writing as the next grammarian writing about Standard English, and no particular fan of Defense Secretary Donald Rumsfeld, but let's just take another look at this news item about the Plain English Campaign giving Rumsfeld its foot in mouth award for "the most baffling statement by a public figure." Here's the paragraph that got him cited:

> Reports that say that something hasn't happened are always interesting to me, because as we know, there are known knowns; there are things we know we know. We also know there are known unknowns; that is to say we know there are some things we do not know. But there are also unknown unknowns—the ones we don't know we don't know.

Now read that carefully. Because my question is, *What the hell is supposed to be wrong with it?*

The quotation is impeccable, syntactically, semantically, logically, and rhetorically. There is nothing baffling about its language at all.

Now, admittedly, I don't know whether it's *true*, but that's a very different matter. What it *says* is completely straightforward: he pays special attention to negative reports because he's conscious of the possibility of areas of ignorance that are not currently recognized as such. His reminder in passing that there are also (i) areas of knowledge that we are aware of possessing and (ii) areas of ignorance that we are aware of seems to allude to a familiar old Persian apothegm:

> He who knows not, and knows not that he
> knows not, is a fool; shun him.
> He who knows not, and knows that he knows
> not, can be taught; teach him.
> He who knows, and knows not that he knows, is
> asleep; wake him.
> He who knows, and knows that he knows, is a
> prophet; follow him.

It also echoes (perhaps unwittingly) the title of Sylvain Bromberger's collection of philosophy papers, *On What We Know We Don't Know*. Bromberger saw it as an interesting epistemological fact that we can be aware of our lack of knowledge in some domain. Rumsfeld is drawing attention to the importance of our unacknowledged areas of ignorance—what we *don't* know we don't know. So what? Is this the best that can be done to identify baffling utterances by public figures, in a world where Judith Butler[1] remains at large, and Michael Jackson's lawyer can say in his client's defense "if these charges were true I assure you Michael would be the first to be outraged"? I don't get it. Hate Rummie if you want for political reasons, but don't try to get grammar or logic on your side. There is nothing unintelligible about his quoted remark, linguistically or logically.

Notes for "No foot in mouth"

1. The reference is to Judith Butler, a Guggenheim Fellowship–winning professor of rhetoric and comparative literature at the University of California at Berkeley, admired as perhaps "one of the ten smartest people on the planet," who was a first-prize winner in the scholarly journal *Philosophy and Literature*'s 1998 Bad Writing Contest. Here is her winning sentence: "The move from a structuralist account in which

capital is understood to structure social relations in relatively homolo gous ways to a view of hegemony in which power relations are subject to repetition, convergence, and rearticulation brought the question of temporality into the thinking of structure, and marked a shift from a form of Althusserian theory that takes structural totalities as theoretical objects to one in which the insights into the contingent possibility of structure inaugurate a renewed conception of hegemony as bound up with the contingent sites and strategies of the rearticulation of power."

LEFT I ON THE NEWS

A Collection of Donsense

http://lefti.blogspot.com/

---

by Eli Stephens

~~Quote~~ Donsense of the day (2/4/2004)

> As Dr. Kay has testified, what we have learned thus far has not proven Saddam Hussein had what intelligence indicated and we believed he had, but it has also not proven the opposite.
>
> —Donald Rumsfeld

And who could argue with that? Indeed, the opposite can *never* be proved, because there will *always* be one more square meter of Iraqi soil which hasn't been dug up to uncover a secret hiding place beneath it. And even if *every* square *milli*meter of Iraq is dug up, Rumsfeld can always argue that, while we were looking, someone moved the "secret stash" from where it was to someplace we've already looked and aren't going to look again.

No one can ever accuse Rumsfeld of failing a course in formal logic. Common sense, definitely. Formal logic, no.

And by the way, what *has* been proved, beyond a shadow of a doubt, is that the claims of certainty and "no doubt" by the Bush and Blair administrations were a complete and utter fabrication. And of course it is those claims on which the justification for "immediate threat requiring preemptive action" (in the realm of international law), or "just war" (in the realm of morality) rest.

~~Quote~~ Donsense of the day (2/10/2004)

> I don't remember the statement [Tony Blair's statement that Iraq had WMD that could be deployed within 45 minutes] being made, to be perfectly honest.
>
> —Donald Rumsfeld

Thanks to Tom Tomorrow[1] for steering me to the quote. Tom also does the heavy-lifting to find this article from last July, which reminds us that Don's boss George made the same statement (which Rumsfeld evidently also doesn't remember):

> The claim, which has since been discredited, was made twice by President Bush, in a September Rose Garden appearance after meeting with lawmakers and in a Saturday radio address the same week. Bush attributed the claim to the British government, but in a "Global Message" issued Sept. 26 and still on the White House Web site, the White House claimed, without attribution, that Iraq "could launch a biological or chemical attack 45 minutes after the order is given."[2]

Donsense of the day (2/25/2004)

Discussing Haiti on *PBS News Hour* last week:

> We have no plans to do anything. By that, I don't mean we have no plans. Obviously, we have plans to do everything in the world that we can think of.

> But we—there's no intention at the present time,
> or no reason to believe, that any of the thinking
> that goes into these things year in and year out
> would have to be utilized.
>
> —Donald Rumsfeld

So if anyone says that Cuba or North Korea or any other country is just being paranoid thinking that the U.S. has plans to invade their country, thanks to Don it's now on record—they do.

The Donald explains the process of democracy in Iraq (4/27/2004)

No, not *that* "the Donald," THE Donald, the one for whom *Left I on the News* coined the phrase "Donsense" to describe his every word:

> **Barbara Starr, CNN:** After June 30, are you in agreement to rule [Ahmad Chalabi] out as a member of the interim government?
>
> **Donald Rumsfeld:** We're not in a position of ruling people in or ruling people out and have no intention to. Clearly, there is a vetting process that's taking place by the United Nations representative Mr. Brahimi, and by the Iraqi people [!!!], and by the Iraqi Governing Council, and certainly the [?] Americans. And they all look at these people and at some point there will be consensus developed in a manner possibly not dissimilar from that we saw in Afghanistan, where there may be some meetings, whether they're public or formal as opposed to informal or not. But their names will be up and someone will rise to the top and somebodies, plural, undoubtedly, given the nature of the country, and that then will be the interim government for a

> period until the constitution is fashioned and elec-
> tions are held sometime next year or the year after
> [!!].

An entire press conference from George Bush? A total waste of time. 145 words of Donsense? Priceless.

More Donsense (tm)? (12/9/2004)

No, just plain bullshit:

> As for the soldier who asked him the question about armored vehicles yesterday, Rumsfeld said, "I don't know what the facts are, but somebody is certainly going to sit down with him and find out what he knows that they may not know, and make sure he knows what they know that he may not know."

If Rumsfeld doesn't know about the severe lack of armored vehicles and their deadly (and crippling) results for U.S. troops, he must be the last person in America not to. And, as has been made clear in other reports (not the one cited), the soldier's superiors are certainly well aware of what he knows; how could they not be? Even Rumsfeld's claim that someone is now going to "sit down with" this soldier and "find out what he knows" is probably bullshit; chances are, if anyone sits down with him, it will be to tell him to shut up in public or suffer the consequences, in the same manner as Sgt. Frank "Greg" Ford, flown out of Iraq strapped to a gurney after being diagnosed for psychological disorders because he reported that his colleagues had tortured Iraqi detainees.[3]

Quote of the Day (belated) (12/28/2004)

> We know that Al Jazeerah has a pattern of playing propaganda over and over and over again. What

> they do is when there's a bomb goes down they grab some children and some women and pretend that the bomb hit the women and the children. And it seems to me that it's up to all of us to try to tell the truth, to say what we know, to say what we don't know, and recognize that we're dealing with people that are perfectly willing to lie to the world to attempt to further their case. **And to the extent that people lie, ultimately they are caught lying, and they lose their credibility**, and one would think that it wouldn't take very long to happen dealing with people like this.
>
> —Donald Rumsfeld, April 2003

The quote above comes from *Control Room*, the documentary about Al Jazeerah which I finally watched last night. Rumsfeld's quote is preceded by a clip of a distraught woman, standing in front of her demolished house, crying out:

> Welcome to my house, Mr. Bush. Look at this. Do you have any humanity? How can you accept seeing a little girl crying for her mother and father? Where is your humanity? Where is your conscience? Where is your God?

Either Rumsfeld is a liar (not much supposition in that statement) or this woman deserves an Academy Award for the best acting job of the year. Of course the clips which accompany Rumsfeld's quote, shots of severely injured and dead children, didn't require much acting.

Notes for "A collection of Donsense"

1. Tomorrow, Tom. "Rumsfeld." *This Modern World by Tom Tomorrow: February 08, 2004 - February 14, 2004 Archives.* 10 February 2004. www.thismodernworld.com/weblog/mtarchives/ week_2004_02_08.html#001322. 5 April 2005.

2. Milbank, Dana. "White House Didn't Gain CIA Nod for Claim On Iraqi Strikes." *White House Didn't Gain CIA Nod for Claim On Iraqi Strikes (washingtonpost.com).* 20 July 2003. http://www.washingtonpost.com/ac2/wp-dyn/A17424-2003Jul19?. 5 April 2005.

3. DeBatto, David. "Whitewashing torture?" *Salon.com News | Whitewashing torture?* 8 December 2004. http://www.salon.com/news/feature/2004/12/08/coverup/index_np.html. 5 April 2005.

N A T H A N N E W M A N . O R G

April 14, 2003

www.nathannewman.org

Privatization of the military

by Nathan Newman

In a proposal for "reorganization" Rumsfeld is seeking to move 300,000 military jobs into the civilian sector and no doubt contracting them out to Bush's corporate allies.

This is all part of an agenda that been encouraging public dollars to push down wages across military-related industries. Just check out this speech by the head of Boeing on ongoing outsourcing there:

> A good example of this was the outsourcing of dining room and food services. In our industry, we were paying aerospace-type wages and benefits to obtain food services, when the food-service industry offered them at a much reduced cost!

But just to really scare you, it's worth remembering who is in charge of privatization at the US Army— none other than former Enron official Thomas White. White has already proposed contracting out 214,000 jobs currently on the government payroll. Just last December, 68 members of the House of Representatives blasted the plan in a letter to White.[1]

Aside from the attack on labor involved in these initiatives, the inherent corruption of massive campaign contributors vying for multi-billion dollar contracts is already obvious in Iraq. But it's worth noting that Army Secretary White had been pushing privatization of military energy facilities when he was at Enron, and then just gaily continued to do so to the benefit of his old company even as he assumed his position heading the Army. Not even a nod to conflicts of interest involved in this selloff to Enron and the other range of companies that were even then ripping off consumers in California.

And the idea that privatization even saves the public money is undermined from evidence across the country. With corrupt deals and the padded salaries of top management, privatization often just lowers wages to the benefit of private industry, not the taxpayer.

Check out these Myths of Privatization[2] or if you have doubts about the Bush administration's real commitment to the taxpayer, read this article[3] about the national challenge to privatization by the American Federation of Government Employees (AFGE) who are sponsoring legislation that only corporate whores would oppose (which means that the Bush administration is opposed).

What would their legislation require? Key elements include:

- requiring agencies to track the cost and size of the contractor workforce (today no one knows how many contractors work for the government or what they are paid);

- ▸ requiring public-private competition (if government employees can do it better for less, let government workers do it);
- ▸ eliminating arbitrary personnel ceilings (when personnel ceilings are too low, managers contract out to get the work done);
- ▸ requiring contracting-in (when contractors fail, bring the work back in-house).

Basically, the legislation says: keep track of how many jobs you are contracting out, see if you are saving money, and if you are not, bring the jobs back into the public sector.

But this is about privatization as ideology, damn the facts. They don't want to track information that might prove their ideology wrong, so they want privatization in a fact-free zone.

Notes for "Privatization of the military"

1. Peckenpaugh, Jason. "Lawmakers blast Army privatization plan." *Government Executive Magazine - 12/20/02 Lawmakers blast Army privatization plan.* 20 December 2002. http://www.govexec.com/ dailyfed/1202/122002p1.htm. 5 April 2005.

2. From the web site of the American federation of State, County and Municipal Employees, AFL-CIO (http://www.afscme.org/wrkplace/ snet05.htm), the seven Myths of Privatization: (1) Myth: Privatization saves money. Reality: Cost overruns are common. (2) Myth: Privatization improves quality. Reality: Quality often declines. (3) Myth: Privatization enhances flexibility. Reality: Privatization ties government hands.(4) Myth: Privatization cuts bureaucracy. Reality: New bureaucratic structures are often needed. (5) Myth: Contracting is fair and rational. Reality: Connections may outweigh qualifications. (6) Myth: Privatization prevents waste and abuse. Reality: Funds are often wasted or misused. (7) Myth: Privatization helps society. Reality: Social goals may suffer under privatization. The "Reality" sections are supported by studies cited on the web page.

3. Schlein, David. "Federal Employee Union Fights Contracting Out." *Labor Notes - Federal Employee Union Fights Contracting Out.* June 2002. http://www.labornotes.org/archives/2002/06/a.html. 5 April 2005.

M A X S P E A K

April 3, 2004

http://maxspeak.org

Taps for mercs

by Max Sawicky

Let's recall the root issue—the sympathy deserved by U.S. contract employees brutally murdered in the line of duty. A lot has turned on the formal definition of "mercenary." To me that's totally irrelevant. I know the definition. They did give me a high school diploma. I've got it around somewhere.

We judge people by what they do. In and of itself, being a contractor reflects no defect of character.

Like some commenters, I happen to think contracting is often an ill-advised public policy, especially in situations calling for the use of force. But the men doing these jobs didn't make the policy or write the laws. All they did was respond to a job offer, as anyone else would do, assuming the risk was tolerable.

Nobody has cited any information that these people were doing bad things, other than serving the U.S. Gov in Iraq. If they are guilty of something for that, then so are all the soldiers. But that's ridiculous.

Some might say these people work for shady companies. I don't doubt it. But let me tell you about my cable company! It sucks! I'd like to lead a team of heavily-armed commandos into their headquarters, and go Robert Kerrey on their ass. Leave no child behind. My life is impacted less by some military contractor with his thumb on the scales than vendors I deal with constantly.

I would say little sympathy would be due a mercenary or, for that matter, a true blue member of the U.S. Armed Forces covertly committing crimes beyond the pale of democratic decision-making. Like the people who worked for Ollie North, for instance. Or people committing crimes right now for Donald Rumsfeld, whoever they might be. I would even excuse some crimes, like blowing up Osama, that may be illegal but really need doing. I'm no purist.

The mercenary outcry has traces of infantile anti-militarism. I'm not accusing any commenters; it's just in the air. It may be exaggerated, but it exists. I appreciate the objections here by some who are themselves veterans, who would clearly not fall into this category.

Soldiers or contractors, all are part of the military proletariat. They are not draftees, but clearly their decisions are the result of limited choices (like everyone else). Special contractors get paid more, but they have less job security (though as we speak, job security for DoD [Department of Defense] employees is deteriorating). I suspect their pay has something to do with the risks they are invited to take. I see no bright line between public employees and contract workers, as far as individual moral worth is concerned. Contract workers cannot be blamed for the policies of the Secy of Defense.

Rulers make the big decisions. Usually others pay the price for those decisions. Focus on the others is deficient politics and flawed moral reasoning. There is no evidence here for any "German following orders" argument. Until somebody reveals those murdered were contracted to strangle Islamicist infants in their cradles, from where I sit they are little different from other military casualties in Iraq.

R.I.P.

THE ROAD TO SURFDOM

March 28, 2003

www.roadtosurfdom.com

It'd be good to be the king

by Tim Dunlop

You know, this democracy thing, it's all such a nuisance really.

Listen to would-be Iraqi founding father, Donald Rumsfeld, at Senate Appropriations yesterday. Senator Byrd has to remind him about all the boring stuff, you know, like accountability, the Congress, the citizens:

> **SENATOR ROBERT C. BYRD** The supplemental request includes $59.9 billion for the Defense Emergency Response Fund. Last year, the Defense Department requested a similar $10 billion reserve fund for operations in Afghanistan. Congress disagreed and worked with you to specify accounts

for funding. Is there a specific reason why such an approach would not work today?

MR. RUMSFELD Senator, because the Congress did not provide the $10 billion that we requested, the Department of Defense had to borrow from other accounts all through October, all through November, all through December, all through January, until we finally got $6.1 billion, thanks to this committee and the Congress, to pay back money that had already been spent. It's just a terrible way to operate. To have to run to other accounts and pull money out and spend it for things you know you're going to have to spend it for is simply not, in my view, a good way to manage our affairs.

SENATOR BYRD Well, Mr. Secretary, I understand it may be a terrible way, but we're talking about the expenditure of the taxpayers' money, and the American people have a right to believe that their money is being spent most prudently. And I know it may be difficult to have to have the taxpayers' representatives in Congress to have to limit — place limitations on the various departments, but this is something that has to be done. We're talking about the liberties of the American people. And it seems to me that we've done very well over the several decades in fighting the wars. There are limitations, there will be limitations, there ought to be limitations. And I regret that you have to live under these limitations, but it's not asking too much of the American people to have their representatives in Congress require the agency heads to answer questions and to place limitations on their spending.

I cite Madison Federalist No. 48: "Power is of an over-encroaching nature"—I'm sorry, I don't have my glasses, but maybe—so it slows me down a little bit. "Power is of an encroaching nature, and it ought to be effectually restrained from passing the limits assigned to it."

Now, Mr. Secretary, I'm sorry you have to labor under these limits, but we've always had them, and we've had wars before, and it's not too much to ask of the department to live within these limitations. Edmund Burke said the people never give up their liberties, except under some delusion. So here we're being asked to give up the people's liberties in the interest of flexibility. Mr. Secretary, I'm against giving additional flexibility. I will give every dollar — I'll support every dollar I can to help the troops and provide for their safety and to help win the war. But to have us extend these limitations to the extent that is being asked here, I just don't—I think it's too much. The reason we have separation of powers is to protect the liberties of the people, and checks and balances and the separation of powers have served the people well now for 215 years. And so count me out when you ask for these additional flexibilities.

I think Congress will respond to the needs whenever the case is made, but we can't afford to give this administration or any other administration a blank check. We didn't give you a blank check when you were secretary of defense in the 1970's, and I don't expect to support giving the blank check to any administration. The people have the right to know how their monies are spent and to believe that they're being spent prudently.

November 24, 2003
www.node707.com

Second class soldiers

by Melanie Mattson

Angry military reservists and their relatives across the country are flooding Congress with complaints about the adequacy of the equipment given to members of the reserves and National Guard in Iraq.

From the San Francisco Bay to Missouri to Cape Cod, lawmakers in both parties are getting an earful from Guard and Reserve members who say they are not properly outfitted for dangerous missions. Outdated or inadequate supplies run the gamut from rifles to Humvees, body armor to night-vision goggles, working radios to Chinook helicopter countermeasures against missiles.

The concerns are resonating on Capitol Hill.

It's just unthinkable we would send any units into a war zone not fully equipped," said Rep. Edward Schrock, R-Va., a member of the House Armed Services Committee and a 24-year Navy veteran who served in Vietnam.

"It's incumbent on this government to provide the reserve units with 100 percent of the same equipment before we send them over there—and obviously they have not done that," Schrock said.

He said that a Chinook unit from Virginia lacked upgraded night vision goggles and radios that could communicate with advanced air warning systems.

"Somebody dropped the ball," Schrock said.[1]

This should enrage every American, regardless if you were for or against the war. This is all part of the "planning" for the war after the war, the planning that never occurred. The Guard and Reserve units routinely live with hand-me-down equipment for training at home, now they've been sent into battle with it.

Read the letters to the editor in *Stars and Stripes*. There are "issues" between the Regular Army and the Guard and Reserve troops, the part-time soldiers resent all the deployments they've had over the last eight years, active duty soldiers resent the bitching; the Guard and Reserve have inferior equipment, but they are getting shot at and dying just like Regular Army.

Further, recruitment and retention, among both regular Army and Guard and Reserve, is now becoming an issue (this was all predictable):

> The US Army Reserve fell short of its reenlistment goals this fiscal year, underscoring Pentagon fears that the protracted conflict in Iraq could cause a crippling exodus from the armed services.
>
> The Army Reserve has missed its retention goal by 6.7 percent, the second shortfall since fiscal 1997. It was largely the result of a larger than expected exodus of career reservists, a loss of valuable skills because such staff members are responsible for training junior officers and operating complex weapons systems.

"The Army has invested an enormous amount of money in training these people, and they're very hard to replace," said John Pike of globalsecurity.org, an independent research group in Washington.

With extended deployments and increasingly deadly attacks by Iraqi guerrillas, Defense Department officials are scrambling to combat a broader downturn in retention and recruitment that they fear is on the horizon.[2]

Enormous damage has been done to national security by this pre-emptive and unnecessary war: the Army, for all intents and purposes is broken and will take years to repair, like after Viet Nam. We've sent our troops into a meat grinder poorly equipped, without basics like ammunition and bullet-proof vests, with radios that don't work, bad night vision goggles, insufficiently armored transport. The poor support planned for the Army and Marines on the ground is both a travesty and a tragedy, and an indictment of the Bush administration. These people are too incompetent to put people in harm's way. If Rumsfeld had any integrity or sense of the value of the lives he places in danger, he should have resigned months ago. That he still has a job tells you how little regard George W. Bush has for our troops.

Notes for "Second class soldiers"

1. Dine, Philip. "Reservists petition Congress for better equipment in Iraq." *KRT Wire | 11/24/2003 | Reservists petition Congress for better equipment in Iraq.* 23 November 2004. http://www.sunherald.com/mld/sunherald/news/politics/7337968.htm. 5 April 2005.

2. Schlesinger, Robert. "Army Reserve battling an exodus." *Boston.com / News / Nation / Washington / Army Reserve battling an exodus.* 23 November 2003. http://www.boston.com/news/nation/washington/articles/2003/11/23/army_reserve_battling_an_exodus/. 5 April 2005.

THE MAHABLOG

August 10, 2003

www.mahablog.com

War and profit

by Barbara O'Brien

As our soldiers suffer in Iraq with inadequate water, food, sanitation, and shelter, President George W. "Bring 'em On" Bush treated his top fundraisers to a private barbeque near his ranch.

The Bush re-election campaign shuttled about 350 top fundraisers to Crawford, Texas, for the event. The favored few had collected $50,000 each for the privilege of chowing down with the President and his advisor, Karl Rove.

But even as he enjoyed the best of Texas cuisine during his month-long vacation, the President assured the nation he is focused on Iraq.

On Friday, the President stood in the driveway of his ranch home with Secretary of Defense Donald Rumsfeld and declared there had been "good progress. Iraq is more secure."

> Mr. Bush would not say whether he shared the assessment of the commander of coalition forces in Iraq, Army Lt. Gen. Ricardo Sanchez, who said Thursday that U.S. forces will remain in Iraq at least two years.
>
> Mr. Bush would only say "I will do what's necessary to win the war on terror." Mr. Bush said Americans have "got to understand I will not forget the lessons of Sept. 11," when America was hit with its worst ever terrorist attack.

> The president also would not say whether he
> had an estimate on how many more soldiers would
> die. Nor did he answer a question on future costs
> of the American presence in Iraq.[1]

It's a good thing he's focused on Iraq. If he were less focused he might forget the war entirely.

To be fair, one reason the President can't estimate cost is that logistics in Iraq became the Mother of All Snafus. Soldiers have lived for months in primitive shelters without windows or air conditioning. Some are without fresh food and showers and telephones and toilets. For a time they weren't even getting their mail. Although news stories say conditions have improved, soldiers continue to write the *Stars and Stripes* and David Hackworth's web site with tales of deprivation.

This soldier wrote to Hackworth in mid-June that troops were so desperate for water they had to purchase water of dubious quality from Iraqis. They also have been short of food. "Soldiers are trying, in vain, to keep mosquitoes from consuming them nightly, and using hoses from an Iraqi latrine stall to get water enough to maintain their hygienic needs," he writes. "There are soldiers, to this day, that live in squalor."

Another soldier wrote,

> While the Army did a great [job] in winning the
> war, what is not being covered is how broke the
> Army logistics system is and the damage it is do-
> ing to the long term readiness and moral[e] of the
> Army. The Army seems to have this NTC rotation
> mentality, which consists of fuck it live in the dirt
> and filth you only have to be here for a month.
> That works at NTC, but it seems no one has

thought of how to sustain an Army in the field for weeks and months at a time.

. . . Our supply lines are clear. There is no excuse why basic health and safety issues and moral issues like mail cannot be addressed. They are not being addressed because the army doesn't know how anymore. Units spend their lives preparing for two-week warfighters and one-month NTC rotations and never think, "okay, how are we going to live out here for six months or a year." It's just not part of the Army's thinking anymore and it's a shame.[2]

This letter from *Stars and Stripes* is dated July 27, 2003:

During the day the temperature reaches 127 degrees in the shade.... Due to a lack of bottled water, each soldier has been limited to two 1.5 liter bottles a day. We've had two soldiers drop out due to heat-related injuries. A person with common sense knows that a normal person can't survive on three liters of water a day."[3]

There's no business like war business

Behind the logistical breakdown in Iraq is a Pentagon team with no personal experience on a battlefield and only a theoretical view of battle. Throughout American military history, most of the work of supplying troops in the field was performed by the military itself. But, beginning in the Clinton Administration, supply and support personnel were shifted into combat jobs and defense contractors were hired to take their place. And, writes David Wood of Newhouse News Service, "This shift has accelerated under relentless pressure from Defense Secretary Donald Rumsfeld to make the force lighter and more agile."

> "When you turn these services over to the private market, you lose a measure of control over them," said [Peter] Singer, a foreign policy researcher at the Brookings Institution, a think tank in Washington. . . .
>
> Thanks to overlapping contracts and multiple contracting offices, nobody in the Pentagon seems to know precisely how many contractors are responsible for which jobs—or how much it all costs. That's one reason the Bush administration can only estimate that it is spending about $4 billion a month on troops in Iraq. White House Budget Director Joshua Bolten said this week he could not even estimate the cost of keeping troops in Iraq in fiscal 2004, which begins Oct. 1.[4]

Can we say, "This is the fault of *management*"? I think we can.

Long-time CEO Rumsfeld and his civilian lackeys are running the military like a corporation. And, as in most corporations, the Suits at the top of the ladder and the worker bees in the cubicles and factories live on different planets. The Suits concern themselves with profits and growth but forget the product. Employees? Employees are *cost*, and employees in Asia work cheaper.

Next we'll hear the Navy is being outsourced to India.

To see clearly what went wrong with logistics in Iraq, look no further than Dick Cheney's old outfit, Kellogg Brown & Root. Last fall the Army hired the Houston-based contractor to draw up the master plan for supporting U.S. troops in Iraq with civilian contractors. But KB&R failed to deliver on its own contracts. The modular barracks, showers, bathroom facilities, and kitchens it had been paid to deliver were AWOL.

Part of the blame lies with the cost of insuring civilians in a combat zone. Rates skyrocketed by 300 and 400% last March as the contractors waited in Kuwait for the war to start. And civilians cannot be ordered to go into a combat zone. Many of them, sensibly, bailed.

'Course, you'd think the well-paid geniuses who drew up the master plan and greedily anticipated record profits from the war would have anticipated this. Guess not.

Warfare 101

Military historian Martin van Creveld defines *logistics* as "minutely coordinating the movements of troops...and supplies...in such a way as to make everything and everybody...appear at exactly the right moment" (*Supplying War*, 1977). Any sensible person can see that military logistics are a little more complicated than running a McDonald's. However, we're dealing with CEOs, so "sensible" is not an operative word. "Greedy," maybe.

(The Bush cartel must've thought the Plan brilliant—outsourcing support and supply would reduce the Pentagon budget and put money into the pockets of some of their biggest campaign contributors at the same time. Win/win!)

According to van Creveld, throughout military history logistics have been nine-tenths of the business of war. Unfortunately, there's no glory in it, and people with a CEO mindset look at logistics and think, *cost*. A common metaphor is the "teeth to tail" ratio. The thinking is that an effective military beast should have more teeth and less tail. Therefore, the military should focus on teeth—the ability to kill—and not waste its time with mundane support details. The problem with this metaphor is that food and water and soap and bug spray and spare parts are not "tail"; they are legs and torso as well, and the beast will die without them.

However, anyone who has done time in a factory or in a honeycomb of office cubicles will recognize the CEO philosophy at work. In business, marketing and finance are the "teeth"; products and the employees who create them are the "tail." *Hi ho, hi ho, to India we go.*

What happened to the professional military? Rummy and his minions have shoved them to the margins. In a recent op-ed in the *Houston Chronicle*, retired Air Force Lieutenant Colonel Karen Kwiatkowski described what she observed during three years of service in the Pentagon. She described functional isolation of the professional corps, who were kept out of the loop of policy decisions; cross-agency ideological cliques who made the real decisions; and groupthink that elevated opinion into "fact."

> Saddam is not yet sitting before a war crimes tribunal. Nor have the key decision-makers in the Pentagon been forced to account for the odd set of circumstances that placed us as a long-term occupying force in the world's nastiest rat's nest, without a nation-building plan, without significant international support and without an exit plan. Neither may ever be required to answer their accusers, thanks to this administration's military as well as publicity machine, and the disgraceful political compromises already made by most of the Congress. Ironically, only Saddam Hussein, buried under tons of rubble or in hiding, has a good excuse.[5]

But last Friday, the Commander in Chief and the Secretary of Defense stood together in Texas, on the other side of the world from the mess they made, and congratu-lated each other on how focused they were and how well their plans were turning out. And, dutifully, the news media reported this.

Fortunately for Rummy, media attention has been diverted to Ah-nold's gubernatorial campaign. The troops in Iraq couldn't get media coverage today if they chipped in and paid for it.

In times like these, I ask myself, WWTD—*what would Truman do?* Harry, I think, would have ordered Rummy to haul his butt to Iraq to straighten out the mess, *now*. Instead, for the next few years we will see armies of consultants who've never set foot on a battlefield make big bucks explaining how to avoid the mistakes of Iraq.

It's the American CEO way.

Notes for "War and profit," "There's no business like war business," and "Warfare 101"

1. "Bush Sees Iraq Progress." *CBS News | Bush Sees Iraq Progress | August 9, 2003 09:06:31*. 8 August 2003. http://www.cbsnews.com/stories/2003/08/09/iraq/main567473.shtml. 5 April 2005.

2. "Hey, Everything Is Just Peachy Keen In Iraq." *SFTT.ORG*. 11 June 2003. http://www.sftt.org/article06112003a.html. 5 April 2005.

3. Bendetti, John, Pfc. "Letters for the week of July 27-August 2, 2003-Heat Casualties." *European and Pacific Stars & Stripes*. 27 July 2003. "htt://www.estripes.com/article.asp?section=125&article=17299&archive=true. 5 April 2005.

4. Wood, David. "Some of Army's Civilian Contractors Are No-Shows in Iraq." *Newhouse A1*. 31 July 2003. http://www.newhousenews.com/archive/wood080103.html. 5 April 2005.

5. Kwiatkowski, Karen. "Flawed decision-making." *Charlotte Observer | 08/01/2003 | Flawed decision-making*. 1 August 2003. http://www.charlotte.com/mld/observer/news/6432709.htm. 5 April 2005.

October 23, 2003

www.tomdispatch.com

Donald Rumsfeld's long, hard slog of cost efficiency

by Tom Engelhardt

Quote of the day (1):

> "The cost-benefit ratio is against us! Our cost is billions against the terrorists' costs of millions." (From Donald Rumsfeld's leaked memo. The full memo is included below.)

Quote of the day (2):

> "It boggles my mind how a memo to four people ends up on the front page of a newspaper," a senior defense official said.[1]

So Donald Rumsfeld is "livid" and a "senior defense official" boggled and we're all deeply shocked that a memo Rumsfeld wrote to a private foursome (Richard Meyers, Paul Wolfowitz, Doug Feith, and Gen. Peter Pace) somehow—this is Washington remember—made it into *USA Today* and then all over the media. Oh yes, and Dave Moniz and Tom Squitieri of *USA Today* report ("After grim Rumsfeld memo, White House supports him")[2] that "three members of Congress who met with Rumsfeld Wednesday morning said the defense secretary gave them copies of the memo and discussed it with them"—Congress being another well-known leak-proof group. Then, according to Fox News, "Privately, defense officials said one of the four officials' staff made photocopies for internal distribution in an attempt to prompt some office-wide thinking. Officials said they believe the memo may have slipped out from someone on that staff, and the assumption for now is that the leak was 'not malicious.'"

Not malicious. Hmmm. The Secretary of Defense essentially attacks his own operation as a slow-witted blunderbuss of an organization ("DoD [Department of Defense] has been organized, trained and equipped to fight big armies, navies and air forces. It is not possible to change DoD fast enough to successfully fight the global war on terror...") and then, having already set up his own separate intelligence outfit, the Office of Special Plans, in the Pentagon, calls for the possible creation of a new counter-terror fighting inter-departmental agency that could move faster. ("...an alternative might be to try to fashion a new institution either within DoD or elsewhere—one that seamlessly focuses the capabilities of several departments and agencies on this key problem.") What would it be called, the mini-Pentagon? The Triangle?

By the way, I love that "seamlessly," another fabulous example of utopian thinking in the Bush administration, and what a great idea in any case, to side-step the slow-moving Pentagon by creating another bureaucratic agency elsewhere. But we always knew that this was an administration for which proliferation was policy.

Rumsfeld then goes on in his memo to paint a gloomy picture of the Iraq and Afghan situations (that "long, hard slog" to success), quite out of whack with the sunny picture of progress being fostered via the administration's new publicity blitz; and offers an analysis of the war on terrorism no less out of whack with the latest administration line on the subject, one that came most recently from no less of an *éminence grise* than the vice president. ("On Monday Dick

Cheney, the US vice-president, told a Republican fund-raising meeting: 'We are rolling back the terrorist threat at the very heart of its power, in the Middle East.'"[3] Next he hands the memo around, knowing that some of his past private memos have also become public property, and then he's "livid" when it leaks.

Throw in the fact that Rumsfeld's name is now at the top of the rumor list for a "resignation" before the 2004 election as well as that the White House recently attempted to take some power over Iraq policy out of his mitts and put it in the none-too-steady hands of Condoleezza Rice, throw in a few factors I can't faintly know about, stir, and you seem to have quite an explosive mix in Washington.

Esther Schrader and Greg Miller of the *Los Angeles Times* offer this insider comment from one of the thousands of unnamed officials of every stripe who pop up at moments like this, now that this administration is leaking like a badly broken dam:

> A military intelligence official said the memo reflected Rumsfeld's rising frustration with events in Iraq as well as a spate of setbacks in Afghanistan, where remnants of the Taliban have regrouped and launched attacks on American troops and the interim Afghan government.
>
> The secretary is also feeling new pressure from the White House, said the official, citing the recent decision to give national security advisor Condoleezza Rice a larger role in managing postwar Iraq. "Why would he be in position to be outmaneuvered" unless there was dissatisfaction elsewhere in the administration? the official asked.[4]

And though it wasn't the line most quoted in the media, you also have the Secretary of Defense talking about the "cost-benefit ratios" of terrorism. Before we're done, we'll have a true soap opera here and before you know it, Don Rumsfeld may actually be morphing into that famed cost-benefit kinda guy, Robert S. McNamara, the Secretary of Defense of Vietnam era fame, who finally cracked and was sent off to run the World Bank by Lyndon Johnson. (A historian friend of mine suggests that McNamara's ghost has long hovered over Rumsfeld's Pentagon.)

Not that I think the gored Secretary of Defense is likely at this point to set up his own "Triangle," nor even an interagency counter-terrorism hut next to the Pentagon, but I do think—whatever may be happening in Iraq—we're seeing this administration slowly fray as the knives come out.

Off on his imperial processional through the tributary states of Asia, the President stopped for a moment to offer "support" for his Secretary of Defense in the form of a meaninglessly bland sentence or two. His traveling party was, however, described by the *Washington Post* as "surprised," as in taken off guard, by the memo. ("Surprised by the release of the document, Pentagon and White House officials sought to depict it as evidence simply of Rumsfeld doing his job to compel the armed forces to adapt to new threats."[5])

. . . Meanwhile, back in Washington, let's not forget that the fertile brain of our Secretary of Defense churned out in that single memo not just one but two new suggested institutions—both evidently imagined as somehow part of his purview. Rumsfeld wants us to consider creating "a private foundation to entice radical madrassas [Islamic schools] to a more moderate course." I have little doubt that it would be named the General Jerry Boykin[6] Foundation for Encouraging Islamic Moderation—or do I mean Conversion? What better way to move the embarrassing general to a new post? The problem, as the "Don" puts it, is: "Does the US need to fashion a broad, integrated plan to stop the next generation of terrorists?"

Ah, that next generation. Perhaps it will be his new mini-Pentagon against a new baby al-Qaeda, or perhaps in his next memo Rumsfeld will call on DARPA [Defense Advanced Research Projects Agency], his advanced R&D outfit, to look into what kind of futuristic weaponry can be created to take out whole new generations of baby terrorists? None of this will be necessary of course if the Boykin Foundation is a hit.

In one of those classic last paragraphs in the mainstream press, Bradley Graham of the *Washington Post* ("Rumsfeld Questions Anti-Terrorism Efforts") ends his piece by picking up the most curious line in the Rumsfeld memo: "In one particularly cryptic line near the end of the memo, Rumsfeld asked: 'Does the CIA need a new finding?' A finding, signed by the president, provides authority to conduct whatever covert activity is stipulated. Rumsfeld did not indicate the covert activity he had in mind."

Rumsfeld and the CIA have been at one another's throats for a while. Schrader and Miller of the *LA Times* comment: "Portions of Rumsfeld's memo seemed aimed at the CIA, giving middling marks to the effort to capture terrorist leaders and raising questions about whether the agency has the authority it needs to do the job."

On the memo itself, Josh Marshall of the talkingpointsmemo.com web site comments on one of its missing elements:

> All this aside, what's missing here, what's troubling about this memo is that it really does seem to be a candid appraisal meant only for his top advisors.

And even in that context there's apparently no sense that any of the key strategic decisions in the war on terror might have been flawed or misguided.

Yes, there's pessimism. But it's pessimism of a certain sort. The theme of the memo isn't that there might have been too much of X or too much of Y, but that they need to consider 2X or 2Y. And perhaps if things get really freaky, Y squared or even cubed.[7]

But let's remember, being in this administration means never having to say you're sorry.

Rumsfeld's war-on-terror memo:

October 16, 2003

TO: Gen. Dick Myers, Paul Wolfowitz, Gen. Pete Pace, Doug Feith

FROM: Donald Rumsfeld

SUBJECT: Global War on Terrorism

The questions I posed to combatant commanders this week were: Are we winning or losing the Global War on Terror? Is DoD changing fast enough to deal with the new 21st century security environment? Can a big institution change fast enough? Is the USG changing fast enough?

DoD has been organized, trained and equipped to fight big armies, navies and air forces. It is not possible to change DoD fast enough to successfully fight the global war on terror; an alternative might be to try to fashion a new institution, either within DoD or elsewhere—one that seamlessly focuses the capabilities of several departments and agencies on this key problem.

With respect to global terrorism, the record since September 11th seems to be: We are having mixed results with Al Qaida, although we have put considerable pressure on them—nonetheless, a great many remain at large.

USG has made reasonable progress in capturing or killing the top 55 Iraqis.

USG has made somewhat slower progress tracking down the Taliban—Omar, Hekmatyar, etc.

With respect to the Ansar Al-Islam, we are just getting started.

Have we fashioned the right mix of rewards, amnesty, protection and confidence in the US?

Does DoD need to think through new ways to organize, train, equip and focus to deal with the global war on terror?

Are the changes we have and are making too modest and incremental? My impression is that we have not yet made truly bold moves, although we have made many sensible, logical moves in the right direction, but are they enough? Today, we lack metrics to know if we are winning or losing the global war on terror. Are we capturing, killing or deterring and dissuading more terrorists every day than the madrassas and the radical clerics are recruiting, training and deploying against us?

Does the US need to fashion a broad, integrated plan to stop the next generation of terrorists? The US is putting relatively little effort into a long-range plan, but we are putting a great deal of effort into trying to stop terrorists. The cost-benefit ratio is against us! Our cost is billions against the terrorists' costs of millions.

Do we need a new organization?

How do we stop those who are financing the radical madrassa schools? Is our current situation such that "the harder we work, the behinder we get"? It is pretty clear that the coalition can win in Afghanistan and Iraq in one way or another, but it will be a long, hard slog.

Does CIA need a new finding?

Should we create a private foundation to entice radical madradssas to a more moderate course?

What else should we be considering?

Please be prepared to discuss this at our meeting on Saturday or Monday.

Thanks.

Notes for "Donald Rumsfeld's long, hard slog of cost efficiency"

1. Reprinted from Fox News. "Official: Rumsfeld 'Livid' Over Memo Leak." *Official: Rumsfeld 'Livid' Over Memo Leak.* 22 October 2003. http://www.veteransforpeace.org/Rumsfeld_livid_102203.htm. 5 April 2005.

2. Moniz, Dave and Tom Squitieri. "After grim Rumsfeld memo, White House supports him." *USATODAY.com - After grim Rumsfeld memo, White House supports him.* 22 October 2003. http://www.usatoday.com/news/washington/2003-10-22-defense-memo-usat_x.htm. 5 April 2005.

3. Borger, Julian. "Leaked memo exposes Rumsfeld's doubts about war on terror." *Guardian | Leaked memo exposes Rumsfeld's doubts about war on terror.* http://www.guardian.co.uk/print/0,3858,4780551-110878,00.html. 5 April 2005.

4. Schrader, Esther and Greg Miller. "Rumsfeld Questions Terrorism Strategy." *Los Angeles Times.* Los Angeles, Calif.: 23 October 2003. p. A1.

5. Graham, Bradley. "Rumsfeld Questions Anti-Terrorism Efforts." *Rumsfeld Questions Anti-Terrorism Efforts (washingtonpost.com).* 23 October 2003. http://www.washingtonpost.com/ac2/wp-dyn/A3217-2003Oct22?language=printer. 5 April 2005.

6. Discussing a battle against a Muslim warlord in Somalia, Lt. Gen. William G. "Jerry" Boykin once said, "I knew my God was bigger than his. I knew that my God was a real God and his was an idol." Boykin, deputy undersecretary of Defense for intelligence, is known for his mixing of religion and militarism.

7. Marshall, Joshua Micah. *Talking Points Memo: by Joshua Micah Marshall: October 19, 2003 - October 25, 2003 Archives.* 22 October 2003. http://www.talkingpointsmemo.com/archives/week_2003_10_19.php# 002106. 5 April 2005.

B O D Y   A N D   S O U L

August 23, 2004

http://bodyandsoul.typepad.com

Another torture memo

by Jeanne d'Arc

> The great thing about *The New York Times* and *The Washington Post* is that you never know where you'll find a front page story.
>
> — I.F. Stone

I suspect Izzy would have recognized one today on page A12 of the *Washington Post*:

> A memo issued last summer by a U.S. Army military intelligence officer appealed for suggestions on how to extract information from prisoners in Iraq and called for tougher means of getting intelligence.
>
> "The gloves are coming off gentleman regarding these detainees," said the memo, which carried the signature of Capt. William Ponce Jr. The source of the memo, who refused to be identified, said it was sent by the intelligence staff of Lt. Gen. Ricardo Sanchez, who was then commander of U.S. forces in Iraq, to all concerned military intelligence personnel in Iraq.

> The memo asked for a list by Aug. 17, 2003, of
> "what techniques would they feel would be effec-
> tive" and could be reviewed by legal experts.
>
> The source of the memo said it was issued about
> a month before the visit to Abu Ghraib by the com-
> mander of the U.S. military's detention facility at
> Guantanamo Bay, Cuba.[1]

Late July or early August. That would be about three
months after Donald Rumsfeld approved a list of 24 interrogation methods for Guantánamo—a list that was later posted
at Abu Ghraib. (General Sanchez specifically approved the
Guantánamo tactics for Abu Ghraib in early September.) It
was Rumsfeld's Undersecretary of Defense for Intelligence,
Steven Cambone, you will recall, who took credit for sending
Miller to conduct an inquiry on interrogation and detention
procedures in Iraq.

The source of the memo is unidentified, and the *Post*
says it couldn't independently confirm its authenticity. But
given the pressures that were building that summer, it seems
plausible. If it's confirmed, it's an enormously important
piece of the puzzle. In April, Rumsfeld approves torture at
Guantánamo. In July, Sanchez's office is talking about
needing more aggressive tactics for dealing with prisoners,
and within a month, the head of Guantánamo arrives for an
"investigation," that, oddly enough, is immediately followed
by adoption of the very methods Rumsfeld approved: Many
of the abuses took place between October and December.

Update: The Wall Street Journal confirms the existence of
the incriminating e-mail:

> Last year, interrogators were under pressure to un-
> cover information about the growing insurgency.

An e-mail sent in July 2003 by a military-intelligence officer on the staff of Army Lt. Gen. Ricardo Sanchez, then the top commander in Iraq, to intelligence personnel said, "The gloves are coming off, gentlemen, regarding these detainees. ... We want these individuals broken."[2]

The e-mail, signed by Capt. William Ponce, recently was uncovered in the prosecution of seven Army reservists charged in the Abu Ghraib scandal. Mr. Ponce, a reservist no longer on active duty, declined to comment. Military officials declined to comment on the e-mail.

Notes for "Another torture memo"

1. Washington Post Foreign Service. "Memo Appealed for Ways To Break Iraqi Detainees." *Memo Appealed for Ways To Break Iraqi Detainees (washingtonpost.com).* 24 August 2004. http://www.washingtonpost .com/wp-dyn/articles/A24822-2004Aug22.html. 5 April 2005.

2. The memo is also reported on here: Oppel, Richard A. Jr. "Army reservist pleads guilty, recounts abuse at Abu Ghraib." *Army reservist pleads guilty, recounts abuse at Abu Ghraib | The San Diego Union-Tribune.* 21 October 2005. http://www.signonsandiego.com/uniontrib/ 20041021/news_1n21abuse.html. 5 April 2005.

L E A N L E F T

December 17, 2003

www.leanleft.com

Rumsfeld: Unindicted co-conspirator?

by Kevin Raybould

I don't ask the question lightly, but I think it is one that needs to be addressed. According to documents recently declassified, the Reagan and first Bush Administrations helped Saddam develop his chemical weapons programs, even though they knew he was using them.

The details will embarrass Mr. Rumsfeld, who as defense secretary in the Bush administration is one of the leading hawks on Iraq, frequently denouncing it for its past use of such weapons.

The US provided less conventional military equipment than British or German companies but it did allow the export of biological agents, including anthrax; vital ingredients for chemical weapons; and cluster bombs sold by a CIA front organization in Chile, the report says.

Intelligence on Iranian troop movements was provided, despite detailed knowledge of Iraq's use of nerve gas.

Rick Francona, an ex-army intelligence lieutenant-colonel who served in the US embassy in Baghdad in 1987 and 1988, told the Guardian: "We believed the Iraqis were using mustard gas all through the war, but that was not as sinister as nerve gas.

"They started using tabun [a nerve gas] as early as '83 or '84, but in a very limited way. They were probably figuring out how to use it. And in '88, they developed sarin."

On November 1, 1983, the secretary of state, George Schultz, was passed intelligence reports of "almost daily use of CW [chemical weapons]" by Iraq.

However, 25 days later, Ronald Reagan signed a secret order instructing the administration to do "whatever was necessary and legal" to prevent Iraq losing the war.

In December Mr. Rumsfeld, hired by President Reagan to serve as a Middle East troubleshooter, met Saddam Hussein in Baghdad and passed on the US willingness to help his regime and restore full diplomatic relations.

Mr. Rumsfeld has said that he "cautioned" the Iraqi leader against using banned weapons. But there was no mention of such a warning in state department notes of the meeting.

Howard Teicher, an Iraq specialist in the Reagan White House, testified in a 1995 affidavit that the then CIA director, William Casey, used a Chilean firm, Cardoen, to send cluster bombs to use against Iran's "human wave" attacks.

A 1994 congressional inquiry also found that dozens of biological agents, including various strains of anthrax, had been shipped to Iraq by US companies, under license from the commerce department.[1]

According to the State Department, that use of chemical weapons constituted a war crime:

> Saddam Hussein seized power in 1979. The list of war crimes and crimes against humanity committed by Saddam Hussein and his regime is a long one. It includes:
>
> - The use of poison gas and other war crimes against Iran and the Iranian people during the 1980–88 Iran-Iraq war. Iraq summarily executed thousands of Iranian prisoners of war as a matter of policy.
> - The "Anfal" campaign in the late 1980s against the Iraqi Kurds, including the use of poison gas on cities. In one of the worst single mass killings in recent history, Iraq

> dropped chemical weapons on Halabja in 1988, in
> which as many as 5,000 people—mostly civilians—were
> killed.[2]

If the use of such weapons was a war crime, and the United States government provided the means to acquire those weapons despite knowing how they were going to be used, does that not make them a co-conspirator? If I give you a gun, or give you the parts to make a gun, knowing that you are going to use it to kill your wife, am I not a criminal?

I do not ask these facetiously, or merely to score points. This question is meant in all seriousness, and I don't think there is a more important question right now: are not former Bush and Reagan officials complicit in Iraqi war crimes? The roots of terrorism are complicated, but it seems clear that oppression plays a large role in creating terrorists. Aiding such oppression helps make the United States a target.

This has to end. I want a real victory in the war on terrorism, not the shallow and pale facsimile of one we seem to be trying to build with creeping police state tactics and random, violent lashing out in the hopes of "remaking" a country or a region or the world with an M1-Abrams and "minimal" civilian casualties. If we are going to have any chance to bring about a real victory, then we must stop pretending that we can talk about democracy and human rights in the daylight and continue to support murdering bastards in the shadows. Everything becomes known, eventually. The world hears not only the pretty words and high minded platitudes, but also the aftermath of the ravages of our puppets and allies. Which do you think they pay more attention to?

Some will argue that supporting people such as Saddam is necessary, sometimes. There is weight to that argument: we live in a bloody, ugly world where the gun is often more powerful than the vote. But when we are faced with such choices we must act in a manner designed to limit the damage. Providing the means to acquire chemical weapons to a man with Saddam's atrocious record is not such a move. There is no one—no one—who could not reasonably expect that Saddam would use those weapons to control his own population if needed. Continuing to provide him the means to acquire chemical weapons after you know he has used them is not a decision designed to minimize the damage. There were other ways to help the Iraqis hold off the Iranians, up to and including direct American involvement on the ground. And if you would say that such a price was too high to pay, then I can only ask why associating the United States with war crimes and attempted genocide was not?

The capture of Saddam provides an opportunity to cleanse Iraq of the past, allow justice to be done, and to create the foundation for moving forward. The same opportunity is now present for the United States. I don't know if Rumsfeld or Schultz or Reagan actually violated any strictures against war crimes. But I do know that there is ample public evidence that they helped provide a monster with the tools of his trade, knowing that he was a monster, knowing that he was using those tools. Let them be indicted, and let them stand before the bar—with the best lawyers they or the American taxpayers (yes, the taxpayers. They were acting in our name, after all) can buy—and explain why they did what they did. It has to end somewhere; why not in a courtroom?

I can think of no better way to write the final lines of this sad, ineffective chapter of American foreign policy. The message to the world and to ourselves would be unmistakable, and its echoes would last for years. No one would be able to doubt then that we believe in the ideals we hold up.

I am not naive enough to believe that this will ever happen. I am not naive enough to even believe that Rumsfeld, Schultz and Reagan will be held accountable anytime soon by the American people. As Jeanne[3] has so eloquently pointed out, the American press simply does not cover these stories in the stark terms they deserve. But the path to victory, the path to a safer tomorrow, requires that men like Rumsfeld be kept as far away from our foreign policy as possible, where they can do no more harm. We may never be able to hold the men in this country who fed the monsters to account, but we can stop them from feeding any more.

Then, and only then, can we start to build a safer future.

Notes for "Rumsfeld: unindicted co-conspirator?"

1. Borger, Julian. "Rumsfeld 'offered help to Saddam.'" *Guardian Unlimited | Special reports | Rumsfeld 'offered help to Saddam'*. 31 December 2002. http://www.guardian.co.uk/Iraq/Story/0,2763,866942,00.html. 5 April 2005.

2. See also this document from the U.S. military: http://www.globalsecurity.org/military/library/report/2000/saddam-hussein_iraq.pdf.

3. Jeanne d'Arc [pseud.]. "The Doctrine of American Infallibility." *Body and Soul: The Doctrine of American Infallibility*. 11 December 2003. http://bodyandsoul.typepad.com/blog/2003/12/the_doctrine_of.html. 5 April 2005.

F A F B L O G

May 26, 2004

http://fafblog.blogspot.com

Fafblog interviews: Donald Rumsfeld

by Fafnir

Fafblog Interview Week continues with our exclusive interview with Secretary of Defense Donald Rumsfeld!

FAFBLOG: Great to have you here Donald Rumsfeld! Lets get right to it an start by askin: what is with this torture thing, and how long have you known about it?

DONALD RUMSFELD: Good gosh, that's a tricky one there. Was it torture? Were detainees indefinitely held for days with bags over their heads? Yes. Were testicles electrocuted? You bet. Were orifices molested, flesh ripped by dogs, and nostrils raped? Almost certainly. But torture? Hard to say.

FB: Wow—that IS hard to say.

DR: It sure is.

FB: A recent article in the *New Yorker* says you approved extending a secret interrogation program that allowed torture tactics to spread to Iraq. Is that true?

DR: My goodness me! Did the Pentagon implement a black ops interrogation program that greatly expanded what guards could do to prisoners? Maybe. Did I personally expand that program to low-level prisoners captured in Iraq? Possibly. Did this lead to the abuses at Abu Ghraib? Who can say?

FB: It's almost like the more questions we ask the fewer answers we know!

DR: The truth is a swirling miasma of shadow and fog, Fafnir.

FB: Now Secretary Rumsfeld, there are a lot of people criticizing your handling of the war over things like the undermanning of the military, the not preparing for reconstruction, the letting crazy militias run whole cities. What is your response to those critics?

DR: Well, jeepers, it's hard to say. It's easy for those people, in their press boxes and their ivory towers, to sit back and criticize without having to do the actual work of running the military. Now would another secretary of defense have done a better job, or do a better job? That question comes with a lot of unknowns. Some of those unknowns we know, and some of them we don't know. Do we have a metric for these known unknowns? Are there more unknown unknowns than known unknowns? Is that another unknown? We just don't know.

FB: It's all so crazy we might as well just leave things as they are with you in charge!

DR: If you say so.

FB: Now we can't let you go without askin you about one more thing. Some people have been sayin you should resign lately... John Kerry, Nancy Pelosi, Tom Harkin, The Economist...

DR: Now, I've accepted responsibility before and I'll accept responsibility again for everything done under my command. But I'll be damned... damned... if I let a few systemic, widespread, and grotesque atrocities reflect on the character and conviction of the high-ranking civilian and military brass who created the environment that fostered those atrocities.

FB: ...*The New York Times, The Army Times, The Seattle Times, The Washington Post* almost, The Council for American-Islamic Relations...

DR: And I'll caution those in the press that they should be very careful about the way they handle and release these stories and these pictures, because right now by piling on the United States they're providing ammunition, aid and comfort to the enemy.

FB: ...Anthony Zinni, Al Gore, Richard Clarke, Wesley Clark...

DR: Thanks for having me here.

M A X S P E A K

August 8, 2004

http://maxspeak.org

More Moore

by Max Sawicky

This post has Steven Den Beste[1] dimensions, so if you have time read on. I attempted a political economic evaluation of *Fahrenheit 9/11* yesterday and by my lights did not fully succeed.

In passing I note that in light of the predilection of the jingoists to seize upon factual inaccuracies, I was on the lookout for any in the film. I only recall one suspect item. The assets of the Saudis in America were estimated at eight hundred and something billion dollars. This was characterized as six percent of the U.S. economy. This would put the total wealth at less than $14 trillion, which is way low. Of course, a measly $800 billion can still open a lot of doors.

More important is the neo-con issue. I went through the entire film without thinking of them or being reminded of them. I do not think this detracted from the content. A plus is that their absence from the story avoided some extra charges of conspiracy-mongering.

How important are the neo-cons? I do not think Richard Cheney or Donald Rumsfeld—the two main drivers for the Iraqi invasion—are neo-cons. I do not think the neo-cons or Israel got us into Iraq. Rummy and Cheney seem to have had some pre-9/11 interest in clobbering Iraq, so the question is why. The only answer goes to oil-based, geo-strategic interests in dominating the region, and to that end, periodically choosing a suitable victim to make an example of.

Of course, the climate after 9/11 afforded them additional, hoked-up excuses, as opposed to genuine motives.

Bush's motives cannot be understood in terms of ideology or strategy, since his little brain is clearly disinclined to venture into those fields. For that our best guide I would say is Maureen Dowd's *Bushworld*, which I discussed previously. On a personal level, she knows her subjects well.

In *Bushworld*, Dowd suggests the operating principles are teen-age rebellion, an Oedipal complex, impulsiveness, and a simple-mindedness that leaves the president vulnerable to multiple-choice-style manipulation by his handlers. 9/11 left Bush amenable to metamorphosis from the neo-isolationism of his presidential campaign to Christian messenger of democracy to the Middle East. This entailed junking his father's habits of consultation, patience, and coalition-building.

The neo-cons' role was to be gasoline on the flames that had already been lit by Cheney and Rummy. They supplied a glorious liberationist rationale for the enterprise. They supplied no compelling political-economic support. What are the neo-cons, really? As far as I can see, they are a bunch of pseudo-intellectual blowhards with great media access and outlets, but no boots on the ground. There is no mass neo-con counterpart to, say, the Christian Coalition. They represent no particular industrial sector. They have magazines, letterhead organizations, web sites, and bloggers. They are like paid entertainers, or court jesters, summoned periodically to deliver a politically convenient message.

In this sense, the whole neo-con/Project for a New American Century thing has been a huge distraction, not to mention a trigger for over-the-top analyses of Israel and Zionism.

Our real ruling elites, or ruling class if you like, seemed to be divided on this war. The elder Bush and Saudi groupies like James Baker or Henry Kissinger looked askance at invasion. (Here again Dowd is useful in reporting that whatever his own views, Poppy Bush is adamant about not interfering in Junior's efforts to be all he can be.)

There is much less disagreement on the "we broke it/we bought it" front. Once committed, the consensus is now that the U.S. must succeed. The elite editorialists of the *Washington Post* and *New York Times* are on permanent patrol of the Kerry campaign, constantly bashing any suggested reservations about the Occupation. Disagreements will hinge on feasibility, and the elites apparently think Iraq is still doable. If Kerry took exception, they would kick his ass.

The naïve political economic view of Iraq is that ownership of oil reserves or competition for oil revenues is the key driver of policy. This does not follow. To begin with, much of the oil revenues are pre-committed to Iraq's creditors, who would have enforceable claims no matter who was running the government. Nothing in this world is more sacred than financial obligations. Otherwise you end up isolated like Cuba or North Korea.

Second, reconstructing the oil industry entails huge contracting costs that reduce feasible net proceeds. Third, another stream of revenue would be fated for the thieves running the government, no matter who they were. So as far as oil booty goes, there is less there than meets the eye.

Oil is an input to production. Production is much bigger than oil. By contrast, the importance of a stable, productive oil industry for supplying the world economy is what really matters. Ownership of oil reserves is secondary. Control of the region is what matters. Periodically, control requires that, as one of the neo-cons noted, you have to throw some little country against the wall. The anti-terrorist motive magnifies this policy, but it is not the source of it.

Cronyism and corruption are readily understandable to the average person. Moore's film foregrounds these factors and in that respect works, and there's nothing wrong with that. But it is not a perspective flowing from fundamental criticism of the way the world works.

At bottom, it's about control of a pivotal resource, and the use of indiscriminate violence on a mass scale to ensure that control.

The emergence of Islamic fundamentalism is one of the fruits of this historic policy, in the following sense. U.S. policy was to prop up disgusting autocrats, rather than risk social-democratic and/or Soviet-aligned regimes. Some of the autocrats survive and prosper by indulging radical Islamism, if not actively boosting it, and stifling any kind of demo-cratic, civil society. Others tried to grind down all opposition from left and right, but were much less successful with

Islamism than with progressive forces. Islamism has gotten the better of some of them (e.g., the Shah), and threatens others (Pakistan, Algeria, Egypt).

Of course, the U.S. supported some radical Islamists directly and lost control of them thereafter.

If you think the anti-Soviet motive justified the policy, then the question becomes why maintain such regimes in the post-Soviet era. By rights, the props for all the monarchist kleptocratic regimes should have been yanked out a decade ago. We might have had some ornery people like Hugo Chavez to deal with, but they would still be compelled to sell us their oil. It's not as if the present rulers of oil-exporting states have afforded their customers a holiday.

In a nutshell, U.S. imperialism in the Middle East/South Asia means regional military domination to ensure the flow of oil. The practice continues to be to err on the side of violence and repression, rather than risk democratic openings. The Iraqi invasion was not necessarily instrumental to this end, hence the elite dispute as to its efficacy. By contrast, the Iraqi Occupation—assuming it is feasible—is presently viewed as important for U.S. prestige, which goes back to domination.

What might have been an alternative? That depends on the point in history in which you find yourself, and what options are therefore available. Presently, past blunders and bad choices limit what is possible now. For instance, condoning Saudi repression has cleared the field of any appetizing alternatives to their rule.

What would a progressive U.S. government do? I suppose we would need to set up a Department of Peace to figure it out.

Notes for "More Moore"

1. The reference is to Steven Den Beste, known for his lengthy blog posts.
   His blog, U.S.S. Clueless (http://denbeste.nu/), is not being updated
   regularly as of April 2005.

H U L L A B A L O O

May 15, 2004

http://digbysblog.blogspot.com/

Black ops

by Digby

Seymour Hersh's latest[1] reveals the existence of a black
operation put into high gear after 9/11 that was stupidly
pushed into Iraq due to frustration and impatience at the
Pentagon.

First, let me say that I am not all that surprised that such
a program existed nor that it was given greater ability to
operate independently after 9/11. As Hersh points out, these
clandestine operations had been used during the cold war
and I certainly assumed that dealing with the asymmetrical
threat of terrorism would probably require at least some
element of high risk spook style activity. It would be naive to
think it wouldn't. In the hands of these unbelievable incom-
petents in the Bush administration it naturally turned into a
complete disaster.

Moral questions aside (and there are many), as the article
details, the problem is that if you use these techniques in
anything but the most secret and rarest of ways and it comes

into the hands of regular people instead of highly trained specialists using real intelligence, then it is not only ineffective in obtaining useful information, it is dramatically counterproductive in terms of compromising long term policy goals.

The CIA sources, perhaps covering their asses, tell Hersh that even they backed off of this stuff when it came to using it against regular people in Iraq. Some in the Pentagon apparently maintain that they had been getting good intelligence on the insurgency using these harsh measures until the "hillbillys" got involved and took pictures, which I find hard to believe. If anything the insurgency got stronger over the period they were sweeping innocent people off the streets and then torturing them in prisons so it doesn't track that they were really getting anywhere. In fact, it looks as if it may have contributed to the US military's problems. If they mean that they managed to get Saddam, I hardly think that was such a big coup. After all, he had terrorized the population for over 30 years so it's not unlikely that someone would have dropped a dime on him eventually.

The fact is that these torture techniques in anybody's hands are a terrible way to get information. People will say anything under torture. I suspect that the "historical information" that General Ripper[2] is so proud of obtaining in Gitmo is probably bullshit. Certainly, after being down there for more than two years those prisoners don't know shit today. Believing their own hype about Gitmo, these people inexorably came to believe that if they just inflicted a little more pain and humiliation in Iraq they'd get the answers they wanted. Meanwhile, bin Laden is still at large and Iraq has blown up into a nightmare.

So, it is a case of macho overstepping and making things worse than they already were, much as the march to Iraq itself was a case of macho overstepping and making things worse rather than better. Evidently, the events of 9/11 released some testosterone rush in the pinched, unfulfilled systems of the ivory tower neocons and they lost the ability to reason and plan.

Hersh's article pretty much confirms that the person who gave the orders to take off the gloves in Abu Ghraib is Don Rumsfeld gofer, Steven Cambone, the man most uniquely unqualified to hold his office since well . . . President Bush. Of course, Cambone being the ultimate micromanager's clerk means that Rummy himself was well aware of everything that went on and approved it.

It's becoming more and more obvious that the White House was intimately involved in these issues, regardless of their plausible deniability. As I point out in my post below,[3] one of the main reasons they wanted to create the "unlawful combatant" designation was to allow unfettered interrogations. The White House counsel, Alberto Gonzales, led that argument. The *Newsweek* article shows that Cheney and Rumsfeld were deeply involved in the Padilla and Hamdi cases and argued forcefully that they (and any other American they deemed a threat) should be considered unlawful combatants, without the protections of even the constitution, much less the Geneva Conventions. They believe in harsh measures without regard to human rights. They have both shown a remarkable propensity to overlook the long term strategic damage of any given decision in favor of some short term emotional satisfaction or political gain.

They knew.

Notes for "Black ops"

1. Hersh, Seymour M. "The Gray Zone." *The New Yorker: Fact.* 15 May 2004. http://www.newyorker.com/fact/content/?040524fa_fact. 5 April 2005.

2. The reference is to the mad General Jack D. Ripper, a character from Stanley Kubrick's movie *Dr. Strangelove: Or How I Learned to Stop Worrying and Love the Bomb.*

3. From the post referred to: "White House counsel Alberto Gonzales openly defends the White House's decision to call the Guantanamo prisoners "enemy combatants" largely because the Geneva Convention would limit their ability to interrogate the prisoners. (It's comforting to know that they promise to operate in Guantanamo in the "spirit" of the Geneva Conventions, though. Trust Us)." (http://digbysblog.blogspot.com/2004_05_09_digbysblog_archive.html#108458601967376557).

C R O O K E D   T I M B E R

May 18, 2004

www.crookedtimber.org

No one left to lie to

by Ted Barlow

Christopher Hitchens has just put up a piece in *Slate*.[1] It's a response to Sy Hersh's most recent *New Yorker* story about the connection between Abu Gharib and Rumsfeld's policies. Here's Simpler Christopher Hitchens:

What Went Wrong: The flaw in Seymour Hersh's theory.

> I, Christopher Hitchens, present Sy Hersh's story as such: Rumsfeld was frustrated at the legal obstacles that (for example) prevented combat forces

from firing at a convoy that they believed contained the Taliban leader Mullah Muhammed Omar. Rumsfeld loosened the rules. The loosening of the rules led to the torture of Iraqi prisoners.

I, CH, believe that this is an incoherent story. There is no necessary link between overruling the combat restrictions that I have highlighted and prison abuse. Furthermore, regardless of the decisions of Rumsfeld, there would still have been bad apples in the military.

Shouldn't opponents of the war have some explaining to do? *Now* they say that the Bush Administration should have killed the leaders of al-Qaeda. I believe that, had the Bush administration taken the steps necessary to take out the leaders of al-Qaeda during major combat operations in Afghanistan, they would have opposed them. Therefore, they are hypocrites.

The struggle against terrorism will be long and difficult. Rumsfeld should treat the soldiers who abused the Iraqi prisoners as traitors and enemies.

P.S. I'd like everyone to look at the bomb with sarin in it, and the uncovery of a mustard gas weapon in Iraq.

If anyone thinks I've misrepresented Hitch, please pitch in in the comments.[2] Because if I understand him correctly, this is a truly shameless piece of misdirection.

The lynchpin of Hitchens' argument, "the flaw in Seymour Hersh's theory," is that Hersh doesn't show a connection between Rumsfeld's policies and torture in Iraq. Hitchens doesn't spend a lot of time on this point, but it seems to be the heart and soul of his case. Here's Hitchens, in his original words:

> Thus, from the abysmal failure to erase Mullah
> Omar comes the howling success in trailer-porn
> tactics at Abu Ghraib. More than one kind of non
> sequitur is involved in this "scenario."

But Hitchens is deceiving his readers. Hersh lays out the connection between Abu Ghraib and Rumsfeld's policies quite directly. Hersh's piece only mentions the combat restrictions as a launching point for his real subject—how Rumsfeld and the Administration loosened the restrictions intended to ensure the humane treatment of Afghan prisoners, and later, Iraqi prisoners. Fred Kaplan summarizes:

> This operation stemmed from an earlier super-secret program involving interrogation of suspected al-Qaida and Taliban fighters in Afghanistan. A memo to President Bush from White House counsel Alberto Gonzales—excerpted in *Newsweek*—rationalized the program by noting that we need "to quickly obtain information from captured terrorists and their sponsors in order to avoid further atrocities against American citizens." This new sort of war, he went on, renders the Geneva Conventions' limitations on interrogating enemy prisoners "obsolete" and "quaint."[3]

This program, Hersh reports, was approved by the CIA, the National Security Agency, and the National Security Council. President Bush was "informed" of it. Hersh also notes that its harsh techniques yielded results; terrorists were rounded up as a result. So, last spring, after Saddam's regime fell in Iraq and Rumsfeld grew frustrated over the failure to find weapons of mass destruction or to learn anything about the insurgents who continued to resist the U.S.-led occupation, he put the same program in motion in Iraq.

That's when all hell broke loose, and conventional prisoners of war—whose wardens had up to that point been following Geneva rules—were suddenly treated like terrorists whose deadly secrets must immediately be squeezed out. Hence, the ensuing torture.

It's impossible that Hitchens didn't know this.

Now, Hitchens might find Hersh unconvincing. He might argue that his sources have lied to him. Or, he might argue that the revised policies about prisoner treatment in Abu Ghraib were still sufficient to ensure the humane treatment of prisoners, and that blame shouldn't flow upward. I can't say that I'd consider these to be good arguments, but at least they're arguments.

Instead, he highlights a detail in the piece, the restrictions that probably prevented the killing of Mullah Omar. He's comfortable defending Rumsfeld's decision to overrule these restrictions. (I would be, too.) He pretends that this story was the heart and soul of Hersh's piece, failing to mention any changes to the rules about the treatment of prisoners. Hitchens asserts that there is no logical connection between these combat restrictions and the torture of prisoners. Well, no. There isn't, *but that's not Hersh's argument.* It's only Hitchens' deceptive cartoon that doesn't make sense.

He caps his piece off with some Michael Moore bashing, saying that opponents of the war wouldn't have approved of techniques that would have led to the capture or killing of al-Qaeda leaders. But *Rumsfeld got what he wanted* in terms of combat overrides. Has Hitchens noticed any outrage among war opponents about that? If so, this paragraph would have been a good place to mention it.

The more I read this, the angrier I get. Who, exactly, does Hitchens think he's fooling?

Notes for "No one left to lie to"

1. Hitchens, Christopher. "What Went Wrong." *What Went Wrong - The flaw in Seymour Hersh's theory. By Christopher Hitchens.* 18 May 2004. http://slate.msn.com/id/2100717/. 5 April 2005.

2. One commenter says this: ". . . quite frankly, I don't find what Hitchens is saying about his political opponents any more nasty then what Hersh's sources (mostly anonymous) are saying about their political opponents," though no comments specifically challenge Ted Barlow's summary point by point.

3. Kaplan, Fred. "Locked in Abu Ghraib." *Locked in Abu Ghraib - The prison scandal keeps getting worse for the Bush administration. By Fred Kaplan.* 17 May 2004. http://slate.msn.com/id/2100683/. 5 April 2005.

FAFBLOG

September 30, 2004

http://fafblog.blogspot.com

Drivin with Donald

by Fafnir

So we're ridin on down the road in our Cross Country Journey of Inner Discovery and Of Course the American Dream when Donald Rumsfeld hits a moose.

"Maybe we should stop an get a tow truck," says me.

"Gosh, that seems pretty excessive," says Donald Rumsfeld. "I mean, was a moose hit? Yes. Do the antlers sticking through the windshield make driving trickier? You bet. But should we just turn around and quit because the road got a little bumpy? I'd say no."

One thing about Donald Rumsfeld that you have to give him credit for is he always cuts through the crap to tell it like it is in his no-nonsense style. I am reminded of this when we hit the second moose.

"Moose happen," says Donald Rumsfeld. "There are moose, and we'll hit 'em. That's the way it goes. We've lost two tires and the brakes. That's life. I'm drunk, legally blind and have been charged with eight counts of vehicular manslaughter in the last three years. Gotta deal with it. Nothing's perfect."

"If you think about it the more moose get hit by us, the fewer moose there are to get hit *by* us!" says me.

"I like the way you think," says Donald Rumsfeld.

Donald grabs a beer an misses a pedestrian. Hooray! One of the moose is still alive an kicks at the engine. "Bad moose," says me. "No beer until you stop." Donald Rumsfeld throws an open bottle a Coors at the back seat to put out the fire.

"Are parts of the car on fire? Sure. Would we like them not to be? Of course. Have I gone insane from three decades of snorting military-grade rubber cement? Quite possibly. Do we need everything to be perfect for us to go out on the road? Well, that's absurd," says Donald Rumsfeld.

"That's very true," says me. "We cannot make the perfect the enemy of the terrible."

The bridge up ahead is either out or doesn't exist. But if we waited for everything to be perfect before we did stuff well then we'd never get anythin done! Forward, onward, downward, Donald Rumsfeld!

Lawsuits: A Chronology

http://talkleft.com

Kuwaiti prisoners mount challenge to detention (October 16, 2002)

by Jeralyn E. Merritt

The *Los Angeles Times* today reports that Kuwaiti detainees at Guantanamo Bay are the first to mount an organized challenge to their detention. They are backed by the Government of Kuwait, an ally of the U.S.

> A dozen Kuwaiti captives have mounted the first organized legal and diplomatic effort by prisoners at the U.S. naval base at Guantanamo Bay to challenge U.S. policy that holds terrorism suspects indefinitely without court hearings or charges being filed against them.
>
> The men assert they are not members of Al-Qaeda, and are merely "charity workers" who were assisting refugees of Afghanistan's harsh regime when they were caught up in the chaos of the war last fall and winter. In attempting to flee across the Pakistani border, they say, they fell into the hands of Pakistanis who "sold" them to U.S. troops, collecting a bounty that American forces were offering for Arab terrorism suspects captured in the region.[1]

The men have been at Guantanamo for a year. No charges have been filed against them. The Government claims they are enemy combatants and not entitled to legal protections.

We remember a year ago when the Government told us that all the Guantanamo inmates were "front-line Taliban or Al Qaeda fighters, 'the hardest of the hard.'"

Later the Government admitted it had not identified any high-level terrorists among them. "Defense Secretary Donald H. Rumsfeld said last spring it is possible that some were "victims of circumstances and probably innocent.... If we find someone's an innocent and shouldn't have been brought there, they would be released."

The Kuwaitis are still here. "They are teachers, engineers and students, according to leave-of-absence documents signed by their employers approving their charitable work. One is a government auditor; another works as a government agriculturist. Some have been fired from their jobs since their capture. Some knew one another before they arrived at Guantanamo."

Their lawsuit is backed by high Kuwaiti officials and has been brought by Shearman & Sterling, a Washington law firm specializing in international law. The prisoners are asking to meet with their families, to be notified of the charges against them, to confer with lawyers and for access to a court or other impartial tribunal.

The Kuwaiti Ambassador has said nine of the twelve have no ties to terrorism. The Kuwaiti government isn't saying all of the men are innocent, but it simply wants the United States to evaluate its countrymen. "Let them be put on trial," Ambassador Sabah said. "If they are innocent, let them go. If they are guilty, we will deal with that. Nothing will solve this issue until they are given due process."

That is unlikely to happen any time soon as the U.S. insists that the men are enemy combatants who may be kept without charges, trials or even military tribunal proceedings until the "war" is over.

The Kuwaitis' lawsuit was dismissed by a federal judge but an appeal is pending in the D.C. Court of Appeals. Oral argument is scheduled for December 2.

British ex-detainees sue Rumsfeld (October 27, 2004)

Four former Guantanamo detainees, now back in Britain, have filed suit against Donald Rumsfeld and others alleging they were tortured in violation of international law. The suit seeks $10 million in damages for treatment it describes as including

> ...repeated beatings, death threats, interrogation at gunpoint, forced nakedness and menacing with unmuzzled dogs, among other mistreatment, during more than two years at Guantanamo Bay.

Lawyers for the men held a press conference today.

> "This is a case about preserving an American ideal—the rule of law," [attorney Eric] Lewis said at a news conference. "It is un-American to torture people. It is un-American to hold people indefinitely without access to counsel, courts or family. It is un-American to flout international treaty obligations."[2]

On a related note, Amnesty International released a report condemning President Bush's response to the 9/11 attacks, which it said has resulted in "an iconography of torture, cruelty and degradation."

Advocacy group to sue Rumsfeld and others over Abu Ghraib (November 29, 2004)

Raw Story reports that the Center for Constitutional Rights, the advocacy group that brought the successful lawsuit in federal court on behalf of the Guantanamo detainees, is ready to strike again. The group will file suit in Germany Tuesday against Donald Rumsfeld, George Tenet and others seeking an investigation into the prisoner abuse at Abu Ghraib. According to the organization's press release:

> In a historic effort to hold high-ranking U.S. officials accountable for brutal acts of torture including the widely publicized abuses carried out at Abu Ghraib, on Tuesday November 30, 2004, CCR and four Iraqi citizens will file a criminal complaint with the German Federal Prosecutor's Office at the Karlsruhe Court, Karlsruhe, Germany. Under the doctrine of universal jurisdiction suspected war criminals may be prosecuted irrespective of where they are located.
>
> The four Iraqis were victims of gruesome crimes including severe beatings, sleep and food deprivation, hooding and sexual abuse. (Further details of the treatment of the complainants will be provided after the filing.)
>
> The U. S. officials charged include Secretary of Defense Donald Rumsfeld, Former CIA Director George Tenet, Undersecretary of Defense for Intelligence Dr. Steven Cambone, Lieutenant General Ricardo Sanchez, Major General Walter Wojdakowski, Major General Geoffrey Miller, Brigadier General Janis L. Karpinski, Lieutenant Colonel Jerry L. Phillabaum, Colonel Thomas Pappas, and Lieutenant Colonel Stephen L. Jordan.[3]

Rumsfeld avoids visiting Germany due to lawsuit naming him (February 04, 2005)

The Center for Constitutional Rights filed a war-crimes lawsuit on behalf of detainees at Guantanamo naming Rumsfeld as a defendant. Rumsfeld isn't taking any chances—he'll skip an important conference to avoid the chance something weird will happen.

In recent days, the Center added Alberto Gonzales as a defendant to the suit. According to this letter,[4] Attorney General nominee Alberto Gonzales's testimony before the Senate Judiciary Committee confirms his role as complicit in the torture and abuse of detainees in Abu Ghraib and elsewhere in Iraq.

Germany refuses to prosecute Rumsfeld (February 12, 2005)

Rumsfeld catches a break in the war-crimes lawsuit filed by the Center for Constitutional Rights on behalf of those abused at Abu Ghraib. It had named Rumsfeld as a defendant and sought to have the German prosecutor file criminal charges against him. Focus English News reports:

> Germany's federal prosecutor will not pursue a criminal complaint accusing US Secretary of Defense Donald Rumsfeld of war crimes in Iraq., reported Deutsche Welle.
>
> Even though a German law requires German prosecutors to investigate allegations of war crimes even if they are not committed by Germans or in Germany, German Federal Prosecutor Kay Nehm said US authorities bore the initial responsibility to do so.

He added that his office could only act if US officials failed to do so, but said this was not the case. A US organization called Center for Constitutional Rights had filed the complaint against Rumsfeld and other high-ranking officials in Germany for the role they played in torture and abuse at Iraq's Abu Ghraib prison.[5]

CCR says the decision is "politically motivated, timed for Rumsfeld's visit and only a temporary setback.

That hasn't stopped the vigilant and determined CCR from proceeding on other fronts. Yesterday they filed a habeas corpus claim in federal court in DC on behalf of 570 Guantanamo detainees.

> The suit, spearheaded by lawyers from the Center for Constitutional Rights (CCR), is captioned "John Does Nos. 1-570 v. Bush" because the Bush Administration has continued to withhold the identities of the detainees it keeps in indefinite detention. Until now, without the names of the detainees and without physical access to them, lawyers have been unable to help those who wish to seek their day in court under the Supreme Court's decision last June in Rasul v. Bush. In that case, also brought by the Center for Constitutional Rights, the Supreme Court held that each detainee has the right to challenge his detention in federal court. Seven months later, the Bush administration continues to disregard the Supreme Court's decision by blocking the detainees from meaningful access to attorneys or the courts.[6]

ACLU sues Rumsfeld over torture policies (March 01, 2005)

Human Rights First and the ACLU have filed suit in federal court against Defense Secretary Donald Rumsfeld over U.S. torture policies.

> The lawsuit was filed in federal court in Illinois on behalf of eight men who were subject to torture and abuse at the hands of U.S. forces under Secretary Rumsfeld's command. The groups charged Secretary Rumsfeld with violations of the U.S. Constitution and international law prohibiting torture and cruel, inhuman or degrading punishment.[7]

Notes for "Lawsuits: a chronology"

1. Serrano, Richard A. "Detainees Launch Legal Step." *Los Angeles Times.* Los Angeles, Calif.: Oct 16, 2002. p. A1

2. Reuters. "Ex-Guantanamo Detainees from Britain Sue Rumsfeld." *US Labor Against the War: Ex-Guantanamo Detainees from Britain Sue Rumsfeld.* 27 October 2004. http://www.uslaboragainstwar.org/article.php?id=6917. 5 April 2005.

3. Center for Constitutional Rights. "CCR Seeks Criminal Investigation in Germany of U.S. Officials for War Crimes in Abu Ghraib Torture." *CCR.* November 2004. http://www.ccr-ny.org/v2/reports/report.asp?ObjID=TCRlT9TuSb&Content=471. 5 April 2005.

4. Center for Constitutional Rights. Letter from Michael Ratner to Bundesanwalt Dietrich. 27 January 2005. http://www.ccr-ny.org/v2/legal/september_11th/docs/Germanletter013105.pdf. 5 April 2005.

5. Source for this story is here: *Deutsche Welle.* "Germany Won't Prosecute Rumsfeld." *Germany Won't Prosecute Rumsfeld | Germany | Deutsche Welle |.* 10 February 2005. http://www.dw-world.de/dw/article/0,1564,1483982,00.html. 5 April 2005.

6. Center for Constitutional Rights. "CCR and Pro-Bono Counsel File Suit on Behalf Of More Than 500 John Does at Guantanamo." *CCR.* February 2005. http://www.ccr-ny.org/v2/reports/report.asp?ObjID=Gock0IFYiv&Content=521. 5 April 2005.

7. ACLU. "The Lawsuit Against Donald Rumsfeld Over U.S. Torture Policies." *American Civil Liberties Union : <font color="#E8E8CD">Lawsuit Against Rumsfeld*[sic]. 1 March 2005. http://www.aclu.org/SafeandFree/SafeandFree.cfm?ID=17572&c=206. 5 April 2005.

L E A N   L E F T

December 27, 2004

www.leanleft.com

Why the defense of Rumsfeld?

by Kevin Raybould

Jeff Cooper highlights something that has me completely perplexed—the steadfast conservative defense of Rumsfeld:

> The president has never liked being questioned. It comes through in his rare press conferences; it came through with stark clarity in his debates with John Kerry. But answering questions is one of the centerpieces of accountability. And to the extent possible, Bush rejects it.
>
> The recent rumblings against Secretary Rumsfeld in the Senate are the first serious sign in a long while that someone may demand accountability from the Bush administration. Rumsfeld's continued presence at the Pentagon has been Exhibit A of the administration's disdain for accountability—Iraq has gone so far wrong, in so many ways for which the Pentagon is responsible, that Rumsfeld's retention of his position simply can't be justified. And yet there he is.[1]

And so many people continue to defend him. Before the war, the air and the blogosphere were thick with talk of cakewalks and flowers at the feet of the soldiers. None of that has come to fruition, of course, and a large part of that failure can reasonably be said to lie at the feet of Rumsfeld. His lack of serious contingency planning damaged—and perhaps doomed—the occupation. His battle plan was too light on troops on the ground. The torture fiasco runs, at least, very high into the Pentagon. The military still hasn't properly equipped its units. Rumsfeld has failed in almost every single respect. If the neo-con dream of rifles bringing Republican-style democracy to the Middle East were ever possible, it is no exaggeration to say that Rumsfeld killed those dreams with his incompetence.

And yet he still remains.

Somewhere, the neo-cons have lost the thread. Perhaps it is because they staked their flag to a man—Bush—who is not mature enough to entertain the possibility of mistake. Angering their patron might result in the end of their influence. Perhaps they see their dreams crumbling and are afraid that if they show dissention or weakness, they will be swept away. Perhaps they have simply lost sight of why you fight the political wars—for the ability to use that power. Perhaps they have gotten so caught up in defeating their political enemies that they have lost the ability to see the larger picture.

Whatever the reason, their defense of Rumsfeld is the neo-cons' greatest failing. I, personally, believe that their plans are naive, show a complete lack of understanding of human nature, and are bound to make the country less safe. But they come by those mistakes honestly, in search of a means to protect the country and better the world. But their defense of Rumsfeld has no such intellectual underpinning. Rusmfeld is obviously bad for their plans and bad for their country. It is harder and harder to defend their support of Rumsfeld as principled in any way. It seems clear that the neo-cons have allowed their politically motivated defense of Rumsfeld to overwhelm their good sense, and thus to place their short-term political goals ahead of their country. And that is unforgivable.

Notes for "Why the defense of Rumsfeld?"

1. Cooper, Jeff. "Accountability." *Cooped Up: Accountability.* 21 December 2004. http://www.jeffcoop.com/blog/archives/002342.html#002342. 5 April 2005.

B O D Y   A N D   S O U L

September 7, 2004

http://bodyandsoul.typepad.com

Connecting the dots

by Jeanne d'Arc

An op-ed in today's *Washington Post* reminds me of something significant that I think has been glossed over: the Schlesinger report on prison abuses in Iraq, Afghanistan and Guantánamo contradicts the Bush administration's claim that the infamous 2002 Justice Department memo justifying torture was only "abstract legal theories" that had no effect on policy. In fact, the Schlesinger report notes, the Defense Department "relied heavily" on the legal reasoning in that memo when it drew up a list of interrogation techniques approved for al Qaeda and Taliban detainees at Guantánamo. The dots are clearly connected between the White House and abuses at Guantánamo. That the same techniques "migrated" to Iraq suggests, but doesn't prove, a connection.

The lack of proof, though, looks less like absence of evidence than lack of interest in asking the right questions. Here are some useful ones, from the same op-ed:

- ▸ Did either the Schlesinger or Army investigations interview officials in the White House or at the Justice Department regarding the February or August 2002 memos relating to the Geneva Conventions and the Convention Against Torture?
- ▸ What role did White House or Justice Department officials play in development of the memos on interrogation techniques signed by Rumsfeld in December 2002, January 2003 and April 2003?
- ▸ Were other agencies—specifically the State Department, which usually takes the lead in interpreting treaties such as the Geneva Conventions and the Convention Against Torture, or the National Security Council—included in the process of developing approved interrogation techniques, and if not, why not?
- ▸ Did guidance from the White House and the Justice Department with respect to the Geneva Conventions and the definition of torture in 2002 contribute to the chain of events in the Department of Defense and military command in Iraq leading to the abuses at Abu Ghraib?

So far, there seems to be a bizarre assumption that the interrogation techniques magically appeared in Iraq. It's sheer coincidence that the administration had previously justified them. The Senate Armed Services Committee will be holding a meeting on Thursday to receive testimony on the Schlesinger report, and they ought to be asking specific questions not only about why torture was approved in the first place, but how, precisely, it "migrated." That doesn't happen by accident.

N E W S   H O U N D S

October 27, 2004

www.newshounds.us

Al Qa Qaa missing explosives scandal continues

by Chris Herrmann

The obfuscation continues on Special Report 10/27 as Bret Baier reports on the Al Qa Qaa missing explosives scandal. We are being overwhelmed with names and dates and conflicting stories, all disguising the fact that while we were busy securing the oil fields we let the explosives get away.

Monday we were told to keep it in perspective—the *NYTimes* reported the missing 380 tons but neglected to put it in context of 400,000 tons found, secured, and destroyed or in the pipeline to be destroyed. (?) So it's "only" 760,000 pounds missing. These are the same explosives of which only two pounds are needed to bring down an airliner.

Yesterday, Tuesday, the existence of the explosives was called into question. The Bush administration can't be held responsible if the explosives were not secured at the site when it was under our control, so the spin for the admin would be to insinuate that the explosives were missing before US troops ever got there. There was even an attempt during the "All-stars"[1] segment to equate massive stockpiles of destructive weapons to WMDs.

Today we hear from Bret Baier that the Pentagon is still analyzing satellite images of the Al Qa Qaa storage facility before the war began, which appear to show large truck activity.

However, this doesn't jive with the facts stated yesterday from Dana Lewis, the embedded former NBC reporter (now a Fox reporter) who said he saw bunkers cracked open by airstrikes, full of weapons, and hangars of rockets, and the bunkers were wired and sealed. (He was travelling with the 101st Airborne, who were ordered to pitstop at Al Qa Qaa on their way to Baghdad April 10, 2003.)

Comment: The US secured the Iraqi oil fields March 22, 2003, three days after we began "shock and awe." I saved the headline. The failure of this administration to prioritize the securing of the known stockpiles of conventional weapons shows extreme disregard for our troops' safety. Whether the theft happened through ignorance, negligence, or plain ol' incompetence, this is more proof positive that Bush is a failure as president and needs to go back to ruining businesses.

Notes for "Al Qa Qaa missing explosives scandal continues"
1. "Fox All Stars" is a Sunday news panel show on Fox News.

CROOKED TIMBER

May 11, 2004

www.crookedtimber.org

Time for him to go

by Ted Barlow

I recently saw a post on a conservative blog asking whether liberal bloggers were going to accept Rumsfeld's apology. I know the answer to this one: *It Doesn't Matter.* The Administration doesn't have to worry about us. They need to worry about what they're doing to minimize the firestorm raging among Iraqis and Muslims. The pictures could hardly have been scripted better to alientate and inflame the people that we'd like to have on our side. Dealing with this terrible stain is of incalculable importance right now.

Donald Rumsfeld has said that he accepts reponsibility, and there are a lot of people arguing that Rumsfeld should resign, not all from the left. Daniel Drezner[1] says that he should resign, in part, because of his poor record of handling postwar Iraq. (So does Dwight Meredith,[2] among others.) *The Economist* says that he should go, in part, because of his arrogant refusal to allow prisoners to be held to the Geneva Conventions, or any standards or oversight at all, created a culture that led to Abu Ghraib. *The Army Times* says that he should resign because of the appallingly poor handling of the reports of prisoner abuse by his office. Jane Galt[3] thinks that only real accountability can help repair the damage. Jacob Levy[4] says that getting rid of Rumsfeld would be an acknowledgment of past error that would improve the Administration's credibility. George Will points out that there are no indispensable men, and gently points out that Rumsfeld's greatest contribution to the War on Terror at this point may be to cease to be the official most identified with it. I very strongly agree. (*Update:* William F. Buckley, too.)

What if, instead, the President and Vice-President decided to tell the world that we owe Rumsfeld a "debt of gratitude," that Rumsfeld is "the best secretary of defense the United States has ever had," and that people should "get off his back." What effect would that have?

Arab commentators reacted with shock and disbe-lief on Monday over President Bush's robust back-ing of Defense Secretary Donald Rumsfeld against calls for his resignation....

"After the torture and vile acts by the American army, President Bush goes out and congratulates Rumsfeld. It's just incredible. I am in total shock," said Omar Belhouchet, editor of the influential Algerian national daily *El Watan*.

"Bush's praise for Rumsfeld will discredit the United States...and further damage its reputation, which is already at a historic low in the Arab world," he added...

What people saw, they said, was the true image of the occupation: humiliation of an occupied people, contempt for Islam, sadism and racism.

"After Mr. Bush's decision to keep Rumsfeld, all their apologies seem like lip service," Dubai-based political analyst Jawad al-Anani told Reuters. "Mr. Rumsfeld would have certainly lost his job if the prisoners were American."

"The United States is spending so much money by setting up Alhurra television and Radio Sawa to improve its image in the Arab world...How can it reconcile that with keeping a man who has in-sulted every Arab through the abuses of Iraqi pris-oners," added Anani, a former Jordanian foreign minister.[5]

Notes for "Time for him to go"

1. Drezner, Daniel W. "Should Rummy Resign?" *danieldrezner.com :: Daniel W. Drezner :: Should Rummy resign?* 11 May 2004. http://www.danieldrezner.com/archives/001281.html. 5 April 2005.

2. Meredith, Dwight. "The Meaning of 'Remain'" *Wampum: The Meaning of 'Remain.'*. 10 May 2004. http://wampum.wabanaki.net/archives/000936.html. 5 April 2005.

3. Galt, Jane. "Time to go." *Asymmetrical Information: Time to go.* 6 May 2004. http://www.janegalt.net/blog/archives/004728.html. 5 April 2005.

4. Levy, Jacob T. "Prediction." *The Volokh Conspiracy.* 10 May 2004. http://volokh.com/archives/archive_2004_05 07.shtml#1084229403. 5 April 2005.

5. Sedarat, Firouz. "Bush's Backing of Rumsfeld Shocks and Angers Arabs." *Bush's Backing of Rumsfeld Shocks and Angers Arabs.* 10 May 2004. http://www.commondreams.org/headlines04/0510-07.htm. 5 April 2005.

FAFBLOG

Thursday, December 09, 2004

http://fafblog.blogspot.com

Transforming: less than meets the eye

by The Medium Lobster

Of late the Medium Lobster has heard many complaints, from the usual leftist quarters, regarding the Bush Administration's retention of Donald Rumsfeld as Secretary of Defense. Few outside the White House have truly appreciated the hard work Secretary Rumsfeld has put into transforming America's military, turning it from a large, cumbersome force slowly bogging itself down in one war after another, to a lighter, faster, smaller, more flammable army capable of losing numerous conflicts simultaneously.

As Rumsfeld pointed out today to a group of sadly uninformed American troops, traditional concepts such as "armor" have become obsolete in today's new and challenging world: "You can have all the armor in the world on a tank and a tank can be blown up. And you can have an up-armored Humvee and it can be blown up."[1] The military of the future can't afford to waste money armoring vehicles that can eventually be blown up, shot up, or gradually broken down by the steady process of natural erosion. That thinking belongs to Old Military—a disdainful, backwards approach to warfare that the United States must cast off in order to succeed across the globe. No, America must turn to the bold, fresh, emerging ideas of New Military, replacing bulky, expensive armor plating with lighter, more efficient designs: papier mache Humvees, chicken wire bombers carrying Styrofoam payloads, folded origami troop transports, and for heavy-duty combat, tanks made entirely of blown glass.

The advantages of such a revolution in military technology and logistics should be apparent to all: a faster, more flexible, lightweight military capable of winning wars fast and losing postwar-occupations even faster, allowing for speedy retreat and redeployment to another invasion. Indeed, with Donald Rumsfeld's New Military, the United States could soon be losing up to three or four wars at once across the globe, failing at its objectives at a record pace. In these new and dangerous times, we can ask no less.

Notes for "Transforming: less than meets the eye"

1. United States Department of Defense News Transcript. "Secretary Rumsfeld Town Hall Meeting in Kuwait." *DoD News: Secretary Rumsfeld Town Hall Meeting in Kuwait.* 8 December 2004. http://www. defenselink.mil/transcripts/2004/tr20041208-secdef1761.html. 5 April 2005.

THE ROAD TO SURFDOM

December 16, 2004

www.roadtosurfdom.com

Friendly fire targets Rumsfeld

by Tim Dunlop

So smiling assassin and neo-conservative poster boy, William Kristol, has attacked Donald Rumsfeld:

> William Kristol, the editor of *The Weekly Standard*, the house journal of the neo-conservative movement, said in an article published on Wednesday that no wartime defence secretary had ever "so breezily dodged responsibility and so glibly passed the buck."
>
> In particular he savaged Mr. Rumsfeld's airy response last week to criticism from soldiers in Iraq over the lack of equipment and resources.
>
> "Surely Don Rumsfeld is not the defence secretary Mr. Bush should want to have for the remainder of his second term," Kristol wrote.[1]

As the rest of the article goes on to note, Rumsfeld has become the target-of-choice for conservatives and pro-war types of various stripes since his stupid answer to a question put to him during a photo-op in Iraq.

Now, no one on the left should get between these suddenly wise members of the pro-war squad as they start to lay the boot into Rumsfeld. Heaven knows, he deserves it. And give him one from me.

But we shouldn't let them get away with merely scapegoating Rumsfeld.

The fact is, virtually everyone in the Bush Administration should be held responsible for the sorts of stuff-ups Rumsfeld is now being so piously chastised for by his own team. Paul Wolfowitz is just as responsible as Rumsfeld for the inadequate troop numbers and underequipped troops, and Colin Powell has been let off way too lightly for his bogus presentation to the United Nations. Vice President Dick Cheney and his office were as responsible as anyone for "stovepiping" the intelligence on WMD and the subsequent "incestuous amplification" that led to a complete stuff up in that regard, while everyone from Paul Bremer, George Tenet and General Sanchez to Condoleezza Rice, Alberto Gonzales and Douglas Feith are all responsible for bad decisions on everything from intelligence to Abu Ghraib.

And what about the clowns—including those inside Kristol's Project for the New American Century—who were championing Ahmed Chalabi as the great Middle Eastern hope, right up until the time he was found to be having some interesting chats with Iran?

The main point to make is this: the reason Rumsfeld's comments were so noteworthy—*you go with the army you have*—is not just because it was offensive to tell the troops to go suck eggs, but because to make such a comment completely ignores the fact that this was a war of choice launched entirely at a time of the Bush administration's own choosing. Thus the level of preparedness was *also* entirely of their own choosing.

Everybody who thought that war *now* was a good idea, argued that we couldn't possibly wait another second longer, and sneered at those who urged a bit more caution—not to mention a bit of actual planning—should be subject to the same blow-torch-to-the-belly that Rumsfeld is now copping.

And obviously that includes the man on whose desk the buck is supposedly meant to stop.

So if Rumsfeld resigns in shame on the back of this friendly fire, good. If he is the only one to go down in shame, then there is still work to be done.

Or put it this way. If Rumsfeld deserves to lose his job, then they all deserve to lose their jobs. And bring it on.

Notes for "Friendly fire targets Rumsfeld"

1. Sidney Morning Herald. "Army friends line up to attack Rumsfeld." Army friends line up to attack Rumsfeld - World - www.smh.com.au. 17 December 2004. *http://www.smh.com.au/news/World/Army-friends-line-up-to-attack-Rumsfeld/2004/12/16/1102787216460.html.* 5 April 2005.

B A G H D A D   B U R N I N G

Wednesday, November 10, 2004

http://riverbendblog.blogspot.com

Rule of Iraq assassins must end . . .

by Riverbend

I'm not feeling well—it's a combination of the change of weather and the decline in the situation. Eid is less than a week away but no one is feeling at all festive. We're all worried about the situation in Falloojeh and surrounding regions. We've ceased worrying about the explosions in Baghdad and are now concerned with the people who have left their homes and valuables and are living off of the charity of others.

Allawi declared a "State of Emergency" a couple of days ago . . . A state of emergency *now*—because previous to this week, we Iraqis were living in an American made Utopia, as the world is well aware. So what does an "Emergency State" signify for Iraqis? Basically, it means we are now *officially* more prone to being detained, raided, and just generally abused by our new Iraqi forces and American ones. Today they declared a curfew on Baghdad after 10 p.m. but it hasn't really made an impact because people have stopped leaving their houses after dark anyway.

The last few days have been tense and heart-rending. Most of us are really worried about Falloojeh. Really worried about Falloojeh and all the innocents dying and dead in that city. There were several explosions in Baghdad these last few days and hardly any of them were covered by the press. All this chaos has somehow become uncomfortably normal. Two years ago I never would have dreamed of living like this— now this lifestyle has become the norm and I can barely remember having lived any other way.

My cousin kept the kids home from school, which is happening quite often. One of the explosions today was so close, the house rocked with the impact and my cousin's wife paled, "Can you imagine if the girls had been at school when that happened—I would have died."

Dozens of civilians have died these last few days in Ramadi, Falloojeh, and Samarra. We are hearing about complete families being killed under the rain of bombs being dropped by American forces. The phone lines in those areas seem to be cut off. We've been trying to call some relatives in Ramadi for the last two days, but it's next to impossible. We keep getting that dreadful busy tone and there's just no real way of knowing what is going on in there. There is talk of the use of cluster bombs and other forbidden weaponry.[1]

We're hearing various stories about the situation. The latest is that 36 American troops have been taken prisoner along with dozens of Iraqi troops. How do people feel about the Iraqi troops? There's a certain rage. It's difficult to sympathize with a fellow-countryman while he's killing one of his own. People generally call them "Dogs of Occupation" here because instead of guarding our borders or securing areas, they are used to secure American forces. They drive out in front of American cars in order to clear the roads and possibly detonate some of those road mines at a decent distance from the American tanks. At the end of the day, most of them are the remnants of militias and that's the way they act.

And now they are being used in Falloojeh against other Iraqis. The whole situation is making me sick and there's a fury building up. The families in Falloojeh have been relegated to living in strange homes and mosques outside of the city... many of them are setting up their families inside of emptied schools and municipal buildings in Samarra and neighboring areas. Every time I see Allawi on TV talking about his regrets about "having to attack Falloojeh" I get so angry I could scream. He's talking to the outside world, not to us. Iraqis don't buy his crap for a instant. We watch him talk and feel furious and frustrated with our new tyrant.

I was watching CNN this morning and I couldn't get the image of the hospital in Falloojeh being stormed by Iraqi and American troops out of my head—the Iraqis being made to lie face-down on the ground, hands behind their backs. Young men and old men... and then the pictures of Abu Ghraib replay themselves in my mind. I think people would rather die than be taken prisoner by the Americans.

The borders with Syria and Jordan are also closed and many of the highways leading to the borders have been blocked. There are rumors that there are currently 100 cars ready to detonate in Mosul, being driven by suicide bombers looking for American convoys. So what happens when Mosul turns into another Falloojeh? Will they also bomb it to the ground? I heard a report where they mentioned that Zarqawi "had probably escaped from Falloojeh". . . so where is he now? Mosul?

Meanwhile, Rumsfeld is making his asinine remarks again,

> There aren't going to be large numbers of civilians
> killed and certainly not by U.S. forces.

No—there are only an "estimated" 100,000 civilians in Falloojeh (and these are American estimations). So far, boys and men between the ages of 16 and 60 aren't being counted as "civilians" in Falloojeh. They are being rounded up and taken away. And, *of course* the US forces aren't going to be doing the killing: The bombs being dropped on Falloojeh don't contain explosives, depleted uranium or anything harmful—they contain laughing gas—that would, of course, explain Rumsfeld's idiotic optimism about not killing civilians in Falloojeh. Also, being a "civilian" is a relative thing in a country occupied by Americans. You're only a civilian if you're on their side. If you translate for them, or serve them food in the Green Zone, or wipe their floors— you're an innocent civilian. Everyone else is an insurgent, unless they can get a job as a "civilian."

So this is how Bush kicks off his second term. More bloodshed.

> Innocent civilians in that city have all the guid-
> ance they need as to how they can avoid getting
> into trouble.

How do they do that, Rumsfeld? While tons of explosives are being dropped upon your neighborhood, how do
you do that? Do you stay inside the house and try to avoid
the thousands of shards of glass that shoot out at you from
shattering windows? Or do you hide under a table and hope
that it's sturdy enough to keep the ceiling from crushing you?
Or do you flee your house and pray to God you don't come
face to face with an Apache or tank or that you aren't in the
line of fire of a sniper? How do you avoid the cluster bombs
and all the other horror being dealt out to the people of
Falloojeh?

There are a couple of things I agree with. The first is the
following:

> Over time you'll find that the process of tipping
> will take place, that more and more of the Iraqis
> will be angry about the fact that their innocent
> people are being killed . . .

He's right. It is going to have a decisive affect on Iraqi
opinion—but just not the way he thinks. There was a time
when pro-occupation Iraqis were able to say, "Let's give them
a chance..." That time is over. Whenever someone says that
lately, at best, they get a lot of nasty looks... often it's worse.
A fight breaks out and a lot of yelling ensues... how can one
condone occupation? How can one condone genocide? What
about the mass graves of Falloojeh? Leaving Islam aside, how
does one agree to allow the murder of fellow-Iraqis by the
strongest military in the world?

The second thing Rumsfeld said made me think he was reading my mind:

Rule of Iraq assassins must end. . .[2]

I couldn't agree more: Get out Americans.

Notes for "Rule of Iraq assassins must end . . ."

1. Many press reports, including *Asia Times Online* ("Terrified Fallujans calling Baghdad tell of A-10 jets raining cluster bombs on the city's streets," Pepe Escobar reported 11 November 11 2004 at http:// www.atimes.com/atimes/Middle_East/FK11Ak03.html), claim that the U.S. military used cluster bombs and chemical weapons in the two major assaults on Fallujah. The chemical weapons charge, anyway, is flatly denied by the U.S. State Department: "The United States categorically denies the use of chemical weapons at anytime in Iraq, which includes the ongoing Fallujah operation. Furthermore, the United States does not under any circumstance support or condone the development, production, acquisition, transfer or use of chemical weapons by any country. All chemical weapons currently possessed by the United States have been declared to the Organization for the Prohibition of Chemical Weapons (OPCW) and are being destroyed in the United States in accordance with our obligations under the Chemical Weapons Convention." From http://usinfo.state.gov/media/ Archive_Index/Illegal_Weapons_in_Fallujah.html.

2. The story referenced in this post is from the Associated Press: Burns, Robert. "Rumsfeld: Rule of Iraq Assassins Must End." *News - Top Stories - Rumsfeld: Rule of Iraq Assassins Must End (AP)*. 8 November 2004. http://news.orb6.com/stories/ap/20041109/us_iraq.php. 5 April 2005.

Donald Rumsfeld: god of modern warfare

by Melanie Killinger-Vowell

I think that those of us who work to keep ourselves well informed would agree that this is an exhausting time to be a news junkie. Everywhere I look, the news is bad. Sometimes I wish that the only news I got was from Fox News, because life would be so much easier! To put it bluntly, sometimes I wish I were dumb enough to believe everything I saw on Fox because my life would be simple, simple, simple and I would think America can do no wrong and all is right with the world.

Dan Senor, the former spokesperson for L. Paul Bremer during Bremer's tenure as administrator of the Coalition Provisional Authority in Iraq, was a guest today (December 21, 2004) on "Your World w/Neil Cavuto." Terry Keenan was the substitute host and she and Senor discussed a range of issues having to do with the war on Iraq.

At the end of their discussion, Keenan asked Senor about Donald Rumsfeld and whether or not "he's become the whipping boy, the whipping boy here? Do you think it's anything more than that?"

Senor replied: "I think Terry we're just coming off a slow news week in Washington and when there's a slow news week people start to seize on non-events. Secretary Rumsfeld will stay put. He should stay put. It's under his watch that two of the most successful military campaigns, Afghanistan and Iraq, the most successful military campaigns in modern warfare, have been conducted."

Feel better now? All is well. Not to worry.

Donald Rumsfeld needs a hug

by Rude Pundit

Donald Rumsfeld is a sad, sad man. How do we know? He said so yesterday at a Pentagon briefing, next to Chair of the Joint Chiefs, Gen. Richard Myers, in an attempt to get Santa to move him from the Naughty list to the Nice one: "I am truly saddened by the thought that anyone could have the impression that I or others here are doing anything other than working urgently to see that the lives of the fighting men and women are protected and are cared for in every way humanly possible." Poor Donald Rumsfeld. Having to bear the burden of the big ol' war on his arthritic shoulders. How could we? Are we not ashamed as Americans to want to beat up this old man?

Look at the picture of him. It doesn't look like he's eating right. His clothes fit him awkwardly. Look through the spectacles and see the recessing eyes of a man who deeply feels the pain of loss. Oh, sure, sure, one might criticize Rumsfeld for having used a machine to sign letters telling families that little Jesse and Janey ain't comin' home for

Christmas, but when you are as sensitive a man as Rumsfeld, how could you handle that? Tears smear ink, you know. But Rumsfeld will sign them now, yes, yes, he will, because those thinning arms must support our demands, our whims, of a Secretary of Defense able to chill his heart so he can sign away life after life after life.

Rumsfeld doesn't know when it will end, he says. Not even after the much vaunted elections. He said, "I think looking for a peaceful Iraq after the elections would be a mistake." Oh, but Rumsfeld will be there, we know. He'll be there after the next Mosul. How it must hurt Rumsfeld to know that a suicide bomber can get inside so very easily. Or maybe he just sighs, sad in his terrible knowledge of what is inevitable. Poor, poor Rumsfeld. He needs a hug.

Maybe he can get one from Dick Myers, standing so loyally next to him, all pretty in his military uniform, bringing it all home by making the following bizarro statement: "This attack, of course, is the responsibility of insurgents, the same insurgents who attacked on 9/11."[1] You may think that Myers is saying that poor Sunnis, afraid of Americans and the Shi'a, coordinated and committed the attacks on the World Trade Center and Pentagon. You may think that Myers is saying that the Saudi terrorists were actually Americans who were rising up against their very own government. But then you would think that you understand Dick, and really, can anyone make sense of what Myers said? Perhaps he's not the best candidate to give Rumsfeld a hug.

Maybe he can get one over at Walter Reed hospital, from an armless soldier, driven mad by his memories of a war about which he has to wonder, endlessly, why he fought, why he was there, why he had to leave those hugging arms behind.

Chances are Rumsfeld will have to go home and turn on video of the first month of war, a fire in the hearth, a cognac on the side table, embracing himself, trying to keep warm in the cold, lonely end-of-year darkness, hugging his body so hard, the sad man who so badly wanted the war.

Thomas Pynchon's epic, absurdist, great big "fuck you" of a novel, *Gravity's Rainbow*, ends with a startling image: we, all of us, the readers of the very book we are holding, are seated in a movie theatre and we're waiting as a rocket, with a young man bound inside, is flying towards our cinema to destroy us all. The book concludes before that rocket completes its journey, but we know that the rocket will fall. It is the nature of gravity.

It's the way the Rude Pundit's been feeling lately, like we're all in this giant movie cineplex, and we're watching some shitty film, and the thing is, we know—hell, we knew from the previews, how the movie's gonna end. And we just keep checkin' our watches, wondering if we could please stop wasting our time and get to the ending already. But above our heads a rocket is at the peak of its arc. It must return to earth. What rises must, indeed, fall.

Notes for "Donald Rumsfeld needs a hug"

1. U.S. Department of Defense News Transcript. *DoD News: Defense Department Operational Update Briefing.* 22 December 2004. http://www.defenselink.mil/transcripts/2004/tr20041222-secdef1861.html. 5 April 2005.

AFTERWORD

THE EAR OF AN AVIATOR: LOOKING AHEAD

BASED ON THE STORY so far, I'll make some predictions about what Secretary Rumsfeld's future will bring:

- We will continue to hear stories about abuse of Defense Department authority. These reports will spring from revelations not of illegal activity, but of activity conducted after consulting lawyers who interpret the law in a certain way to justify the activity. This is what happened with the torture memos. This is what happened with the Strategic Support Branch, the spy unit Rumsfeld created with no Congressional oversight. Who knows what we'll hear of next?

- We'll continue to find out more about how ideology, more than intelligence, drives Rumsfeld. Here I'll put it bluntly: Rumsfeld's record shows a clear disregard for reporting that contradicts his belief system. Two glaring examples spring to mind: notice Melanie Mattson of *Just a Bump in the Beltway* expressing her anger and frustration with the military not providing proper equipment for Reserve and Guard troops fighting in Iraq. The article she points us to describes outdated or inadequate equipment that "run[s] the gamut from rifles to Humvees, body armor to night-vision goggles, working radios to Chinook helicopter countermeasures against missiles." Now notice that Mattson is writing her post in November of 2003, a little over a year before Specialist Thomas Wilson posed his famous question to Rumsfeld. As Eli Stephens of *Left I on the News* put it in his post on December 9, 2004: "If Rumsfeld doesn't know about the severe lack of armored vehicles and their deadly (and crippling) results for U.S. troops, he must be the last person in America not to." Another example is the justification for the Iraq invasion itself. Rumsfeld said, referring to Iraq's weapons of mass destruction: "We know where they are. They're in the area around Tikrit and Baghdad, and east, west, south and north, somewhat," leaving no room for interpretation. This despite intelligence reports that used far more reserved language, and U.N. Inspector reports that failed to find any weapons of mass destruction at all. Other examples include his expectations for the number of troops required to occupy Afghanistan and Iraq and his publicized expectations for the length of U.S. involvement, despite contradictory expectations from other military experts. So far, the consequences of

Rumsfeld following his ideology have not been fatal to his career. Others, however, have paid a price.

- Lawsuits will continue. Jeralyn Merritt of *TalkLeft* has been tracking them, as shown here, and there's no reason to believe we've seen the end of them. The people filing these suits are victims of torture by Rumsfeld's military, and so far, Rumsfeld has been immune, but it really is just a matter of time before these stories congeal into a coherent narrative that elevates Rumsfeld to the status of full-blown war criminal. As the pseudonymous blogger Holden Caulfield of *First Draft* put it in March 2005, while pointing out that there is no statute of limitations on war crimes: "If German war criminals can be prosecuted sixty years after their crimes were committed, so can American war criminals. Someday, there will be war crime trials. Perhaps in a truly Free Iraq."

- Rumsfeld will resurface as a major media event. It happened at the beginning of the Iraq invasion and occupation, it happened when the Abu Ghraib torture scandal broke, and it happened after Specialist Wilson asked The Question. It's impossible to predict what event will trigger it— it's probably safe to say that it won't be anything so mundane as a war crimes charge or accusations of profligate spending—but it is also easy to predict that in this news cycle, Rumsfeld will not be painted in a positive light, and a new round of criticism and calls to resign will ensue. Do I need to add that bloggers will be busy?

Of course, this collection paints a particular picture of Rumsfeld, but since I do not think history will be kind to Rumsfeld, I offer all of this as a record of what we know now, and what has been said about it. Rumsfeld had trouble hearing another question that day in Kuwait, just after fielding the question from Specialist Wilson. He might have been stalling for time. "Your voice was dropping off on me and I've got an aviator's ear," he said, asking to have the question repeated. As more challenging questions come to Rumsfeld, that aviator's ear might come in handy.

THE BLOGGERS
(IN ORDER OF APPEARANCE)

Tim Dunlop (The Road to Surfdom)

Tim Dunlop is an Australian writer currently living in Washington D.C. His Ph.D. dealt with the role of intellectuals and citizens in public debate and it was this work that led to his interest in blogging. *The Road to Surfdom* first went to air in May 2002 and quickly became Australia's most widely read left-leaning blog.

Geoffrey K. Pullum (Language Log)

Geoffrey K. Pullum is Professor of Linguistics at the University of California, Santa Cruz, where he served as Dean of Graduate Studies and Research from 1987 to 1993 and was named Distinguished Professor of Humanities in 2004. He is author of a book of humorous and satirical essays on the study of language (*The Great Eskimo Vocabulary Hoax*, University of Chicago Press, 1991) and co-author (with Rodney Huddleston) of *The Cambridge Grammar of the English Language* (Cambridge University Press, 2002). He has written for *Language Log* since its foundation in 2003.

Eli Stephens (Left I on the News)

Eli Stephens is the proprietor of *Left I on the News*, on the Internet since 2003.

Nathan Newman (NathanNewman.org)

Nathan Newman is director of Agenda for Justice, an organization that provides legal and policy support for unions and other grassroots organizations working to enact progressive legislation. With a Ph.D. in Sociology (University of California, Berkeley) and a law degree (Yale), he has written extensively on labor and policy issues, including his book *Net Loss: Internet Prophets, Private Profits, and the Costs to Community*. He also runs *NathanNewman.org*, one of the most popular online blogs with an emphasis on workers' rights issues. He was formerly associate counsel at the Brennan Center for Justice in its Poverty Program. His email is nathan@ nathannewman.org.

Max B. Sawicky (MaxSpeak)

Max Sawicky is an economist at the Economic Policy Institute. He has worked in the Office of State and Local Finance of the U.S. Treasury Department and the U.S. Advisory Commission on Intergovernmental Relations. He also serves on the at-large national board of the Americans for Democratic Action.

Melanie Mattson (Just a Bump in the Beltway)

Melanie began her blogging career as a weekend guest poster at *Daily Kos* in October of 2003. From there she went on to found *Just A Bump in the Beltway* on November 15 of that year.

A 20-year resident of the D.C. metropolitan area, this musician-turned-writer and theologian received a master's degree in theology from the Washington Theological Union in spring 2005.

Barbara O'Brien (The Mahablog)

Barbara O'Brien is the proprietor of *The Mahablog*. She has been posting her commentary there since 2002.

Long ago, Barbara earned a bachelor's degree in journalism from the University of Missouri. Since then—when she wasn't raising very small children or finessing a mid-life crisis—she has enjoyed, in her own words, "a long but unremarkable career in the book publishing industry, in various capacities."

Her journalism career has been rekindled by the popularity of her blog and other blogs she contributes to, including *Buzzflash, Alternet, Democratic Underground, Scoop,* and *Open Source Politics.*

She is the author of *Blogging America: political discourse in a digital nation* (William, James & Co., 2004).

Tom Engelhardt (TomDispatch.com)

An editor in publishing for the last 30 years, Tom is the author of *The End of Victory Culture: a history of American triumphalism in the Cold War era.* He is at present consulting editor for Metropolitan Books, a fellow of the Nation Institute, and a teaching fellow at the journalism school of the University of California, Berkeley.

Jeanne d'Arc (Body and Soul)

Jeanne is the founder of *Body and Soul*, on the Internet since the summer of 2002. In 2003, she received the Koufax Award for Best Writing.

Kevin Raybould (Lean Left)

Kevin Raybould contributes to *Lean Left*, on the Internet since 2002.

Fafnir (Fafblog)

No stranger to politics, Fafnir played small but critical roles in the Bush, Clinton, and McCheese administrations throughout the 1990s. Over the years he has served as a clown, a drug czar, a bicycle, and the state of Oregon. He currently lives in a blimp in the sky with his co-blogger Giblets and their sidekick, Pope John Paul II.

Digby (Hullabaloo)

Digby, recipient of the Koufax Award for Best Writing in 2004, is the founder of *Hullabaloo*, on the Internet since 2002.

Ted Barlow (Crooked Timber)

Ted Barlow is a regular contributor to *Crooked Timber*. He has been blogging since 2002. He lives in Houston with his fiancee and crime-solving dog.

Jeralyn E. Merritt (TalkLeft)

Jeralyn E. Merritt is a Denver attorney in private practice representing persons accused of serious federal and state offenses. She served as one of the principal trial lawyers for Timothy McVeigh in the Oklahoma City Bombing Case.

Ms. Merritt is a past Secretary and Treasurer of the National Association of Criminal Defense Lawyers. She is co-author of a text on the U.S.A. Patriot Act and has testified before both Congress and the United States Sentencing Commission on drug sentencing laws. From 2001 to 2003, she was a Lecturer in Law at the Denver University College of Law teaching Wrongful Convictions and Criminal Defense.

Ms. Merritt lectures nationally on a variety of legal and political topics, and has been a television legal analyst since 1996, most frequently appearing on Fox News and MSNBC.

Ms. Merritt is also the creator and principal author of the award-winning weblog, *TalkLeft: The Politics of Crime*, providing liberal coverage of crime-related political and injustice news. *TalkLeft* has won the Koufax Award for Best Single Issues Blog 2002–2004. Since its inception in 2002, the site has welcomed more than 5 million visitors.

Chris Herrmann (News Hounds)

Chris Herrmann was one of the Fox News researchers for Robert Greenwald's exposé *Outfoxed: Rupert Murdoch's War on Journalism*. She continues to monitor Fox News at *News Hounds* ("We Watch Fox So You Don't Have To").

The Medium Lobster (Fafblog)

The Medium Lobster is a higher being whose ultimate essence transcends the bounds of what you call "space" and "time." He appears, for the benefit of your limited perception, to be a medium lobster.

Riverbend (Baghdad Burning)

Riverbend has been writing her blog *Baghdad Burning* from Baghdad since 2003. She is the author of *Baghdad Burning: girl blog from Iraq* (The Feminist Press at the City University of New York, 2005), which was adapted for the stage and produced in March 2005 by Six Figures Theatre Company in New York City.

Melanie Killinger-Vowell (News Hounds)

Melanie Killinger-Vowell was one of the Fox News researchers for Robert Greenwald's exposé *Outfoxed: Rupert Murdoch's War on Journalism*. She continues to monitor Fox News at *News Hounds* ("We Watch Fox So You Don't Have To").

Rude Pundit (The Rude Pundit)

Rude Pundit is the founder of *The Rude Pundit,* on the Internet since 2003.